God's Influencer

ABOUT THE AUTHOR

Father Michael Collins is a priest of the archdiocese of Dublin. He has written several books on church history, art history, the Bible and several biographies. His books have been translated into 15 languages.

God's Influencer

A Short Biography of Carlo Acutis

Fr Michael Collins

Published by
Red Stripe Press
Upper Floor, Unit B3
Hume Centre
Hume Avenue
Park West Industrial Estate
Dublin 12
Ireland
email: info@redstripepress.com
www.redstripepress.com

Cover photo © The Carlo Acutis Centre, used with kind permission.

Paperback ISBN 978-1-78605-229-2
ePub ISBN 978-1-78605-230-8

Typeset by www.typesetting.ie

Printed in Dublin by SPRINTBOOKS

I dedicate this book to my mother, Helen, in gratitude for the life and faith which she gave me.

Contents

PREFACE

Biographies about teenagers are rare. Rarer still if the teenager died at the age of 15. On the bridge of childhood and adulthood, there is little to relate. The seed of life is barely sprouting and life has yet to blossom. So, why write a biography of a life cut short and why read such a life?

In the case of the young Carlo Acutis, his fifteen years were similar to those of many of his age group, yet during his short life he won the affection of his family and many who came in contact with him. It is highly unusual for the memory of a deceased person to grow and indeed a cult to develop. Yet this phenomenon has happened to Carlo Acutis.

Within a year of his sudden death in October 2006, people who had known Carlo approached the priests of his parish with memories and stories of his holiness. The parish priest spoke with Carlo's mother, Antonia, who confirmed that her son had indeed shown signs of tremendous faith and religious zeal. The priest contacted the Archbishop of Milan, Cardinal Tettamanzi, who advised waiting for a period to see if these unusual accounts would continue. They increased and, after seven years, Cardinal Tettamanzi authorised an investigation into not only Carlo's life but also reports of miracles due to his intercession.

Carlo Acutis' life was cut short in his early teens, before he had time to mature. Yet his religious faith and sensitivity to sick people and people living with money problems shows a young man mature before his age. As his story unfolded, people both in Italy and across the globe learned of an extraordinary young man who achieved much and influenced many. In time, he would be known as God's Influencer.

INTRODUCTION

Two saints were born in London, three miles and two centuries apart. The first was baptised a member of the Church of England and became a highly respected academic at the University of Oxford. The second was born to Italian parents working in London. The first converted to the Catholic Church in middle age, became a cardinal and died when he was 89. The second was baptised Catholic but his life was interrupted by sudden death at the age of 15.

The two, one an elderly cleric and the other a boy on the crest of youth, are worlds apart, both figuratively and chronologically. Yet the old man and the teen were united in their Catholic faith, and their tangible affection for Jesus, His mother and the host of sinners and saints which make up the Christian churches.

John Henry Cardinal Newman, born in 1801, was a controversial figure in Victorian England, reviled by some former co-religionists and hailed by many Catholics who welcomed his conversion to their faith. Carlo Acutis, born in 1991, was baptised in London's chic West End but just four months following his birth was brought by his parents to their native Italy where he lived out the rest of his short life.

Each in their own way enriched the Catholic Church and the wider world in which they lived. Newman spent his life embroidering words with his elegant pen while Acutis harnessed a new world wide web to share the richness of the faith in God whom St Augustine of Hippo described as "ever ancient, ever new".

Newman's story has been well-known for two centuries. The short path of Acutis' life is only now unfurling to audiences across the globe who are fascinated by the genial young man who grasped the mystery of God in the palm of his hand before he was called beyond the horizons of this world.

Both are venerated for their simple sanctity and their transparent piety. Once citizens of London, they have both gone, in Newman's words:

"To rest forever after earthly strife,
In the calm light of everlasting life."

1.

The story of Carlo naturally begins with his parents, Andrea Acutis and Antonia Salzano. Andrea was born on 6 February 1964, a native of Turin, into a prosperous family. His early education was in Italy, and as a young man he studied political economy at the University of Geneva in Switzerland. Two years after his graduation, Andrea enrolled in the Italian army for a 24-month term of military service. At the time, all eligible men were obliged to serve either in a defence branch or the equivalent in social service in a volunteer capacity. Andrea joined the Alpine corps of the Italian army and was stationed at Aosta, in the north of Italy. He was later transferred to Rome, where he was assigned to the Cesare Battisti barracks of the Carabinieri, or police force.

In the summer of 1986, Andrea visited the seaside resort of Forte dei Marmi on the northwest Mediterranean coast as part of his annual leave. During this visit, he met a young girl, Antonia Salzano, who was visiting from Rome. Over the course of the summer their romance developed. When his military service came to an end, Andrea moved to London to work at a bank. Andrea's father, Carlo Sr, was a highly successful entrepreneur who ran a family insurance brokerage, and the opportunity to work in one of the most important financial capitals of the world was due to both family connections and his clear talents. Antonia decided also to transfer to London, enrolling in a master's programme in publishing and economics. Thus, the pair could develop their relationship while also pursuing their chosen careers.

The couple decided to marry. Andrea was offered a position with the Lazard Brothers financial firm as a consultant. The couple quickly settled in London and, by now fluent in English, decided that they would live in the British capital, at least in the short term.

Andrea and Antonia married at the Basilica di Sant'Apollinare in Rome on 27 January 1990. The newlyweds returned to London the next day, postponing their honeymoon to a later time when they could arrange to have a week or more. They delayed the decision on a destination, as work was pressing and holidays could wait until the summer. Arriving in London in the middle of winter, the newlyweds moved into a ground floor flat at 4 Gledhow Gardens, a nineteenth-century townhouse set in the fashionable and affluent suburb of Chelsea. The flat overlooked a large square park, filled with mature trees and shrubs, and was flanked by the Old Brompton Road and Wetherby Gardens. A few blocks to the north of Gledhow Gardens lay Hyde Park and two miles to the east was Buckingham Palace, the royal city residence of Queen Elizabeth II. This was not only in the centre of London, but it was in the most affluent and attractive part of the city.

In the autumn following their marriage, Antonia became pregnant. A sociable person by character, Antonia soon had a circle of friends with whom she spent the days while Andrea worked in the City, an hour away by public transport. He left the house each morning at 7.00 a.m. and returned home twelve hours later.

The months went by in a flurry. Preparations were made to welcome the child and Antonia and Andrea spoke often by phone to their extended family in Italy, who awaited news of the birth. International phone calls, made from fixed land-lines, were expensive but, as an only child, Antonia was anxious to speak with her parents and friends as often as was practically possible. Sometimes the calls were to ask for advice during the pregnancy; other times simply to ward off homesickness. Finally, on 3 May 1991, their first child was born in the prestigious Portland Hospital. He was named after his paternal grandfather when, two weeks later, on 18 May, the infant was baptised Carlo Maria Antonio at the Church of Our Lady of Dolours Servite parish on Fulham Road. The parish priest, Father Nicholas Martin OSM, could have had little inking that the infant whom he welcomed into the Christian community of the Church would achieve so much in a short life.

As Antonia and Andrea intended to spend some weeks during the summer in Italy, the baptism was to be a small family occasion. The summer would provide opportunities for the extended family and friends to see the new arrival. Both sets of grandparents came to London for the baptism, and Luana, his maternal grandmother, undertook the responsibility of godmother to the newborn, while Andrea's father, Carlo, undertook the role of godfather. During the ceremony, the infant Carlo was dressed in a long, white, embroidered lace gown which had been in the family for generations.

In Italian society, baptism is something automatically given to infants, and the ceremony is usually followed by an elaborate meal and party. Neither Andrea nor Antonia were particularly committed to their Catholic faith and before the birth of little Carlo, Antonia had only been to Mass on the occasion of her first Holy Communion, her Confirmation and her wedding. In that, she and her husband were little different from the vast number of Italian Catholics for whom cultural practice and faith are so closely intertwined. Andrea, whose parents attended church more regularly, had also accompanied them to various religious ceremonies.

The London chapter ended abruptly in the summer when a position came up in Andrea's father's firm. Andrea resigned his position at the London bank in order to return to Italy. On 8 September, the contents of their home were packed up and little Carlo and his parents boarded a plane bound for Milan.

For Antonia, the return to Italy allowed her to connect with her family and friends in Rome as well as establish new bonds in Milan. The early months were taken up by settling into a new home and caring for her infant son. Andrea had to make a rapid transition, learning the ropes in his father's office and meeting the increasing number of clients under his care. The full working day meant an early start each morning and a late arrival home. The main family time together came at the weekends, when the trio visited the parks of Milan and attended Sunday lunch with relatives and extended family. Occasionally during the summer, the couple made excursions to the surrounding countryside or the mountains north of Milan, where they spent the afternoon walking. Andrea's responsibilities increased considerably when, on 1 January 1992, he was appointed director of Vittoria Insurance.

Milan, Italy's wealthiest city, with a population of over 1 million inhabitants, is the seat of the national stock exchange. It is a centre of the arts, tourism, the fashion and publishing industries, and chemical production. Milan is the administrative centre of Lombardy, one of twenty regions in Italy, and, with some ten million inhabitants, by far the most prosperous. In the 1990s the population of the region was augmented by the arrival of immigrants from Romania, Albania and Africa.

Antonia decided, shortly after the family's return to Italy, to engage in the world of publishing, for which she had trained in her father's footsteps. Although it was a part-time position, she required help in minding her young son. The family hired a young Polish girl, Beata Spercznska, who was to remain with them for four years. Beata was to play a seminal role in the religious development of the boy in her care. The young nanny was part of the large Polish community which had settled in Italy in the decades following the election of Karol Wojtyła as Pope John Paul II in 1978. Poland had endured severe economic hardship under the Communist regime, which had been in power since the end of the Second World War. The return of Pope John Paul II to his homeland in 1979 for a brief visit encouraged some Poles to challenge the government's social policies. The following year, a shipyard worker, Lech Wałęsa, proposed a strike against work conditions. From this act of defiance grew a populist movement, *Solidarność*, which led firstly to martial law and contributed in part to the collapse of Communism in Eastern Europe in 1989.

Despite the change in Poland's government, large numbers of Poles chose to search for work abroad where pay and conditions were better than in their native land. Italy, with its Catholic heritage, was a popular destination, made all the more attractive by the presence of the charismatic Polish pontiff.

It was in large part due to Beata's influence that the young Carlo began to develop a religious faith. When she took him for a walk, she invariably visited the churches that they passed. The young child was fascinated by the beautiful buildings and chapels which he visited daily.

On outings to the local parks, the young child collected flowers and blooms which he placed in front of statues and images of the saints in the churches. He also insisted on lighting votive candles, a common practice in Catholic and Orthodox churches, to accompany his prayers. Beata had a number of small prayer cards with images of Our Lady linked to her homeland. Of these the best known was the celebrated Black Madonna of Częstochowa, a Marian shrine situated in the monastery of Jasna Góra in southern Poland. Carlo kept these images in his bedroom, and when his parents put him to bed at night he asked them to pray with him. Beata gave little Carlo a silver medal with images of Jesus and Mary, which he wore around his neck throughout his life. Antonia initially found her son's requests to pray at bedtime uncomfortable as she had only a basic religious education, and religion had not played a significant part in her life. Nonetheless, to satisfy her son she recited the most familiar prayers, and joined with him as he mentioned all the family and friends who were important to him. Carlo also asked to hear stories from the Bible and for his parents to tell him about the saints, and to satisfy his requests they purchased a Bible suitable for children and some lives of the saints written for young children.

When his mother took him for walks, he insisted that they visit each church they passed. In 1994 the family moved to a new apartment in the city centre. The apartment on the fashionable nineteenth-century Via Ludovico Ariosto was elegantly appointed and filled with antiques. Beata remained with the family to help them settle, but it soon was time for her to move on to obtain a profession. Antonia and Andrea's work commitments increased and so, in December of the following year, they hired a young Mauritian, Rajesh Mohur, to help with cooking, cleaning the apartment and helping the young Carlo. Rajesh had migrated to Italy in the mid-1980s in the hopes of finding stable work. The son of a Brahmin pandit, or Hindu priest, Rajesh's original plans to study for a master's degree in England were not realised as following his father's sudden death he was obliged to return to Mauritius to help support his family. After a period at home, the young man decided to emigrate in search of a better future.

Rajesh settled in Milan and found a number of temporary jobs before he was taken on to look after the young boy and the household. Rajesh had graduated with a degree in physics from a university in the northern Indian state of Rajasthan. But as a migrant to Italy, his academic opportunities were limited and he sought work which would allow him stay long-term in Italy. The first challenge was to change his temporary permission to live in Italy to a permanent visa. In addition to looking after the apartment, Rajesh would accompany the child to school and collect him when lessons ended in the early afternoon. Along with Carlo's parents, Rajesh was the closest person to the young boy, spending the next ten years with him at home. A bond of trust grew between the two. Carlo's facility for maths and physics may have stemmed in part from Rajesh's help and encouragement with homework.

2.

The same year that Rajesh came to work for the family, 1995, Carlo was enrolled in the nearby Parco Pagani, the community pre-school, where he learned the basics of reading and writing. Each morning Rajesh accompanied the boy to the school and in the early afternoon collected him to bring him home. As the pair made their way to and from the school, Carlo noticed a considerable number of people sleeping on the streets. As he lived in a comfortable apartment, he could not understand why so many people seemed to be outcasts of society.

There was little remarkable about the young Carlo. With his other school companions, he learned the rudiments of reading, writing and simple arithmetic. The school day was short, finishing before lunchtime, giving Carlo the opportunity to return home for his midday meal. In the afternoons, he often continued to meet friends to play in a local park, while on occasions friends came to play at his house, or he visited the homes of other school companions. This was generally the type of life that many privileged young children had in the prosperous city, but, as an only child, Carlo may have appreciated the company more than most.

Even as a young child, Carlo was inquisitive. He continued to develop a fascination with his religion, asking his mother complicated questions for a five-year-old boy. Antonia, who had rarely visited a church before the birth of her son, realised that she knew quite little about the Catholic faith. She laughing referred to her son as "my little Buddha" as he appeared wise beyond his years. In later years, she added another title to her son. "When I look back on Carlo's life, I realise that he was my saviour."

The death of his maternal grandfather, Antonio Salzano, after a short illness at the age of 58, came as a shock for the whole family. Antonia, as the only child, took on the administration of the family publishing business, a responsibility which required her absence from home and regular travel both in Italy and abroad. With his father's absence for work as well, Carlo found himself increasingly relying on the care of Rajesh.

In September 1997, at the age of six, and having completed two years at the pre-school near Parco Pagani, Carlo enrolled at the Institute of San Carlo on the Via Lanzone, beside the Basilica of Sant'Ambrogio which houses Leonardo da Vinci's celebrated Last Supper. The institute had been founded in 1844 by the Ursuline Sisters, who continued to teach and administer the popular school. Although he was happy in the school, after three months, Carlo's mother decided that, for practical reasons, it would be easier if he attended the nearby Institute of San Tommaso, administered by the Sisters of St Marcellina. Young Carlo barely noticed the change and, when he enrolled in January 1998, he quickly made friends among his class and schoolmates.

The nuns and staff at the school noticed something unusual about Carlo. Not only was he a kind and sensitive child, but he was also very spiritual. He prayed often, asking God, through Mary and the saints, for the needs of people he knew. Although he came from a well-off family, he lived simply and showed little interest in expensive clothes or toys. He may have been unaware of how much his parents provided for him, assuring him of everything he needed as well as holidays and trips abroad. The teachers noticed that Carlo was very attentive to the needs of other children. While most young children, even in group settings, are focused on themselves, Carlo sought to help his classmates who were in difficulty. In his first year in the school, he realised that children made their first Holy Communion at about the age of 10. Carlo asked his parents if it would be possible to make his Holy Communion earlier. He was just 7.

The request of the child was unusual and Carlo's parents spoke with the teacher, who did not object to the boy receiving the sacrament earlier than was customary. His mother asked a priest whom she knew, Fr Emillio Carai, for his opinion. He spoke with Carlo and realised that the boy was not only determined but sincerely wished to receive first Holy Communion as soon as possible. Fr Emilio was pleased to find a child who was so eager to receive the sacrament. In recent years, first Communions had become occasions where parties and elaborate lunches had over-shadowed the spiritual aspect of the sacrament. Fr Emillio, who was by now a good friend of Carlo's parents, encouraged the young boy to make his request to receive his first Communion in the early summer. Dispensation for his young age was granted by Archbishop Pasquale Macchi, who had served for several years as private secretary to Pope St Paul VI (1962–79) and who had now retired to spend his last years in the Romite Monastery of Sant'Ambrogio at Perego, a short distance outside Milan. Carlo was permitted to prepare for the reception of the sacrament of Penance and Reconciliation, followed by his reception of Holy Communion.

A few weeks after his first Confession, on 16 June 1998, Carlo made his first Holy Communion at the Monastery of Sant' Ambrogio at Perego. As was the custom, he wore an ankle-length white alb and a wooden cross around his neck for the ceremony. The cloistered nuns were both curious and pleased to see such a young child make the request to receive his first Communion.

The Mass was followed by a meal with his extended family and later a party for his friends and school companions. There was an abundance of gifts, including various religious objects to commemorate the event. Among these was a statue of Our Lady, a prayerbook for children, an illustrated Bible, a book on the lives of the saints, and religious medals. The gift which most attracted him was a rosary, a set of fifty beads which Christians have used for centuries to meditate on the life of Jesus and His mother, Mary. The young boy decided to recite the rosary every day.

While some thought that this pious phase would soon pass, it was the beginning of an unusual fascination with and appreciation of the Eucharist which was to mark

Carlo's life. He vowed to both attend Mass daily when possible. With rare exceptions he was able to keep his spiritual promise.

As several parishes in Milan have evening Masses, the young child was accompanied by his mother, grandmother or Rajesh to the local church before returning home for supper. During the summer holidays, when he spent several weeks with his maternal grandparents near Salerno in the southwest of Italy, the local priest and a small group of parishioners were surprised and pleased to see the young child attend Mass each evening. For decades religious practice had steadily declined in Italy, and, while some still attended Sunday Mass, barely a handful took part in the daily Mass which was celebrated in every parish. Some weeks following his first Communion, Carlo began the practice of writing a diary. Rather than record events of the day, the young boy began jotting down thoughts, a practice which he continued and developed until the end of his short life. In the diary, which was found after his death, the young Carlo wrote, "This is my life plan. To live for and with Jesus."

Carlo's parents were quizzical about their son's interest in religion. Both at school and on his visits to the local churches he learned more about the saints. A particular incident fascinated him concerning three Portuguese children.

From May though to October 1917, a group of three Portuguese children claimed to have seen the Blessed Virgin Mary. The children – Francisco de Jesus Martin (10), his sister Jacinta (9) and their cousin Lúcia dos Santos (7) – were minding sheep on the outskirts of the village of Fatima when the first apparition took place. Over the following months, the apparition of the woman took place on the thirteenth day of each month. Two of the children died within two years, while Lúcia became a nun.

In 1941 Sr Lucia claimed that in 1917 she and her cousins had seen a vision of hell. She wrote about the visions they had seen in her memoir, published that same year. The first and second visions were published in her memoir, but the third part of the vision was transmitted to the pope and not revealed until 2000 by Cardinal Joseph Ratzinger, elected five years later as Pope Benedict XVI.

The story of the children and the Marian vision made a strong impact on Carlo, who doubled his resolve to live a good life. He was fascinated to learn that Pope John Paul II had narrowly survived an assassination attempt on 13 May 1981, as he entered St Peter's Square, shortly before meeting pilgrims. A Turkish terrorist shot the pope several times, seriously injuring the pontiff. Writing of the event some years later, Pope John Paul II noted, "one hand pulled the trigger, but a maternal hand guided the bullet from killing the target."

The biography of a mid-nineteenth-century Italian saint from nearby Piedmont also captured Carlo's imagination. St Dominic Savio was one of ten children in a poor family. At the age of seven he received his first Communion. On that occasion the youth wrote in his diary that he wished to receive the sacrament of Penance regularly and Holy Communion when possible, to foster a friendship with Jesus and Mary, and to choose death rather than sin. Dominic's life was cut short when he died on pleurisy in 1857 at the age of 14.

Dominic's memory did not die. Many recalled his good nature and cheerful disposition. St John Bosco wrote a short biography, as he had known the boy. Devotion to St Dominic was widespread not only in Italy but across the world. What attracted Carlo was Dominic's appreciation of the Eucharist.

However, the saint who made the greatest impact on Carlo was the national saint of Italy, Francis of Assisi. Born in the Umbrian town of Assisi in 1182, Giovanni di Bernardone was the son of a prosperous cloth merchant. His mother, Pica, may have had French origins, for which reason the young Giovanni was given the nickname Franceso, the little French boy. When the young man was twenty, he was conscripted into a local army which engaged the nearby town of Perugia in battle. Wounded during a skirmish, Francesco was taken prisoner and remained captive for a year before his release. After months of recuperation, Francesco tried to enlist in the ongoing battle between the pope and the Holy Roman Emperor but failed to gain a commission. Around this time, he had a dramatic change of heart, and, rejecting violence, he devoted himself to the care of the poor and outcasts.

Francis, the name by which Francesco became known, took some cloth from his father's shop and sold it in the nearby town of Foligno. His father was infuriated when his son gave the money to the priest at the church of San Damiano, where Francis claimed to have had a vision of Jesus asking him to rebuild the semi-derelict church.

Brought before the local bishop, whom his father hoped would talk sense to his son, Francis took off all his clothes and gave them to his father. He claimed that he had come into the world naked and would live by God's providence. To the amazement of the bishop and assembled crowd, Francis walked out of the town naked and lived for a while in woodland outside the town.

Francis enlisted sympathetic friends to help him restore the stone church of San Damiano, where he claimed to have heard the voice of Jesus coming from a painted wooden crucifix. He also repaired the nearby church of Santa Maria. He became increasingly convinced that he should live a simple life, devoted to the poor and in particular the lepers who lived in isolation from the townsfolk. In 1208, Francis formed a band of followers who were impressed by his zeal and desire to live a relatively simple life. Along with his companions, he spoke in public about religion. Several clergy were skeptical as they regarded his knowledge of religion basic, but Francis managed to obtain approval from Pope Innocent III for his band of followers to adopt a community rule. Two years later the brothers, or friars as they were known, set up frugal living quarters and began a new way of life. They wore simple clothes, often made from castoff garments, and each day some of the friars visited the public town square where they spoke about their religious faith.

The brothers were entirely different from monks and nuns who lived in monasteries and convents, away from the public. Their chosen task was to pray to God for themselves and for others. The friars, on the other hand, met people and helped them in a practical way. The transformation in the lives of the townsfolk was remarkable, and led to a renewal of spirituality.

Women's role in medieval society was largely confined to the home, where they acted as mother and spouse. Those who were unmarried had similar restrictions. Feudal society was complex and had developed largely from the ruins of the Roman Empire. While some elite women could own and administer property, such women belonged to a select minority. One of the earliest followers of Francis was Chiara ('Clare' in English) Offreduccio, a noblewoman of the town. Inspired by the friars' radical way of living, Clare and some female companions decided to live in the convent of San Damiano, supporting the friars by prayer and solidarity. As the friars grew in number, so did the convents of nuns. Clare obtained permission from the pope to found convents where her sisters could live a life of poverty, relying on providence and the generosity of neighbours.

The example of saints like Francis made an impression on the young Carlo, and when his parents bought a house in Assisi he was able to make regular visits. In particular, Carlo loved to visit the Basilica of St Francis, dating from the early thirteenth century, which was decorated with enormous frescos by the artist Giotto, depicting the life of St Francis. On 26 September 1997, a violent earthquake badly damaged the town and surrounding countryside. At the height of the tremors, part of the vaulted frescoed ceiling collapsed in clouds of dust. The church was closed for a long period and several of the frescos were damaged. Eleven people died during the earthquake and some 70 percent of the houses in the town were evacuated and shuttered. Two years were to pass before the church was restored, at the cost of millions of euro, and tourists and visitors were once more allowed enter.

Yet over ten thousand inhabitants of the town and surrounding villages remained in makeshift accommodation.

St Francis and St Clare were not the only saints who attracted the young Carlo's attention. While visiting his family in the south of Italy, he had heard about the brave efforts his maternal great-grandfather, Renato Salzano, had made in helping Jews escape German troops during the Second World War. He was fascinated to hear of Giuseppe Placido Maria Nicolini, the bishop of Assisi between 1928 and 1973. During the Second World War, the bishop and his secretary, Don Aldo Brunacci, assisted thousands of refugees who came to the town and district of Umbria. Among those searching for help were more than two hundred Jews, who were marked for deportation and death if the Nazi invaders should find them. Within months, scores of Jewish relatives joined those who had found shelter at Assisi.

The bishop enlisted the help of the clergy, especially the Franciscans who administered the churches and shrines of the hillside town. The informal rescue mission was called the Assisi Network, and was specifically aimed at helping and sheltering Jews. The bishop took the religious objects which might identify the Jews if they were caught and hid them in the basement of the episcopal residence. He gave the owners coded references so that when the war ended they could reclaim their possessions. Father Rufino Niccacci, the Franciscan guardian in charge of the Convent of San Damiano, forged documents to provide the Jewish refugees with false identities and arranged for their accommodation in 26 friaries and convents in Assisi. Thanks to this act of deception, all of the Jews who took refuge in Assisi escaped the searches of the German soldiers.

Monsignor Giovanni Battista Montini, one of the closest assistants of Pope Pius XII, and later to be elected as Pope Paul VI, oversaw similar rescue missions throughout Italy. The future pope housed Jews in his country residence, an extra-territorial space where the Germans could not enter. The friars and nuns of Assisi helped the Jews obtain kosher food and assisted them in preparing for the celebration of Passover and food to end the fast of Yom Kippur.

Over the course of two years, some three hundred Jews were saved thanks to the Assisi Network and, after the war, Father Niccacci set up a cooperative to assist Jewish and Christian victims of the war in the district of Montenero on the outskirts of Assisi. Carlo, who delighted in heroic tales, was particularly impressed by the bravery and determination of the people who helped the persecuted Jews.

Of all the contemporary saints, Carlo was most taken by Padre Pio of Pietrelcina in the south of Italy. For many Italian Catholics, the Capuchin friar was one of the most popular characters and stories abound of his sanctity.

Francesco Forgione was born in 1887 in the town of Pietrelcina in the southern Italian province of Benevento in the district of Campania. As a young boy of 15, Francesco entered a Capuchin friary at San Giovanni Rotondo. He was later ordained a priest, and, in accordance with the tradition of the time, he changed his baptismal name to Pius. Henceforward he was known as Father Pius, or Padre Pio in Italian. His life would have been unremarkable were it not for a phenomenon which occurred in 1918. While praying one September afternoon in the chapel, the young man experienced excruciating pain in his hands, side and feet. Soon these were to develop into weeping wounds, similar to those displayed by St Francis of Assisi, of whom the Capuchins were followers. This manifestation was referred to as the stigmata, whereby those inflicted bore physical wounds similar to the crucified Christ.

Following investigation into the phenomenon, the Holy See prohibited Padre Pio for some time from regularly celebrating Mass in public. Despite the prohibition, crowds continued to visit the friary in the hope of catching sight of the friar with the bandaged wounds. The sanctions were finally lifted in 1933. Despite authorising several investigations in the alleged stigmata, the Holy See remained ambivalent until Pope Paul VI lifted all restrictions in the mid-1960s, shortly before the friar's death in 1968. In 1982, the Archdiocese of Manfredonia authorised the opening of Padre Pio's cause for beatification, a process which ended in 1999 with the ceremony of beatification at the Vatican. Just four years later, on 16 June 2002, Blessed Pio was canonised by Pope John Paul II in St Peter's Square, in the presence of more than a quarter of a million participants.

These tales fired the imagination of the young Carlo, who collected books on the lives of the saints. But Carlo was not satisfied simply to read about these inspiring Christians. He wanted to imitate their example as best he could.

Rajesh recalled how after Christmas one year Carlo gathered up toys that his grandparents and family had given him and brought them to a local park where he sold them and then asked Rajesh to distribute the money to poor people who were sleeping in the open in front of the local church.

On another occasion, Carlo visited the local park with his grandmother. The Filipina helper of a local family began to speak with Carlo's grandmother, telling her of a tragedy which had befallen the family. When he returned home, Carlo opened a box in which he had saved money and the next time he saw the young woman he gave her all that he had collected.

Rajesh was deeply impressed by not only Carlo's generosity but also by his piety. Although Hindu, Rajesh joined Carlo in reciting the rosary before he went to sleep. After four years observing Carlo, Rajesh decided to become a Catholic. Antonia and Andrea were surprised by their assistant's decision but in 1999 Rajesh was baptised in the parish church of Santa Maria Segreta. But Carlo's influence did not end there. When Rajesh's mother visited her son in Milan she was a guest of the Acutis family. Although she did not understand Italian, Carlo spoke with her in English. He suggested that she might like to visit Lourdes, and, with his father's help, Rajesh's mother visited the French shrine. She too converted to the Catholic faith.

Rajesh further recalled that although he was supposed to look after the child as well as cleaning, shopping and cooking for the family, Carlo was very independent. As he grew up, he was increasingly aware of all that Rajesh did for the family. To save him from the task of keeping Carlo's room, the young boy got up early each morning to make his bed and leave his room tidy.

It was Rajesh's help which Carlo enlisted when, as a very young boy, he wanted to buy a sleeping bag for a poor man whom he met on occasions in the district. Like many young people, Carlo kept a small, locked box in which he kept loose coins and his pocket money. Having counted out his savings, Carlo and Rajesh went to a nearby shop where they bought a sleeping bag for the man who was sleeping rough. Rajesh recalled the great satisfaction which Carlo felt.

But that was not sufficient, and, a short time later, Carlo purchased more sleeping bags for people who were sleeping fought around the Porta Sempione district, not far from the family home. The same criteria applied with food. When Rajesh was preparing the evening meal, Carlo asked him to add in extra so that later they could bring a warm meal to people nearby. It was not a question of leftovers. He insisted that the food be the same as the food the family ate. At first Rajesh was entrusted with the task of bringing the food to the people, but, as Carlo grew up, he took over the responsibility.

Around the age of eight, Carlo began putting on weight. The source was food. He had a particular weakness for a chocolate spread, popular in Italy, called Nutella. In addition, he loved ice cream. His parents pointed out that he needed to watch his weight and be careful about his health. Reluctantly the young boy followed their advice, making a virtue out of the sacrifice. But that in turn was helpful when he noted that his mother was also gaining weight. He suggested a diet and found better food for her. He also insisted that she join him every day when he took their four dogs on a walk in the local parks. In later life, Antonia would look back in gratitude on these excursions with her son, when the two could converse uninterrupted.

One of Carlo's earliest friends, Mattia Pastorelli, recounts an occasion when, during the summer vacation of 2001 in the Umbrian town of Assisi, the two boys decided to buy an ice cream. They had first met when they were about six years old and Mattia was visiting his grandfather. The two friends went to fetch an ice cream in a shop several streets away. It was a hot afternoon and, having chosen their flavours, the children began the climb back to the house. As they were walking, Carlo noticed that the change in his hand seemed more than it should be. Pausing to count the coins, Carlo discovered that he had been given 20 cents extra by the shop attendant. Realising the error, he insisted on returning to the shop to give back the extra coins. When Mattia complained that it was hot and that the money could be returned the next day, Carlo explained that the figures for the day's sales had to be calculated each evening and balanced. He did not want to cause the assistant any inconvenience and so, despite the heat, the two returned. The young attendant was surprised when the boys entered the shop and Carlo cheerfully explained the mistake.

Several members of Carlo's family identified a particular streak in his character. From his earliest years he was very sensitive to the needs of others. Being an only child may have made him more attentive to other children his own age. His parents, aware that he had no siblings and was prone to being spoilt, fostered his attempts to make friends. It was common practice for friends to meet one another outside school, sometimes for birthday parties or simply to play in the local public parks. But on occasion, Carlo asked his mother if he could invite some children home to play and usually stay for early supper. Antonia paid little attention and readily agreed. But Carlo told his parents and Rajesh about the children he invited. With few exceptions, the children he invited were in some type of difficulty. Their parents may have had problems or be going through separation or divorce. Some young friends suffered with depression and psychological problems. Carlo clearly believed that by befriending them he could help them cope with challenging situations. His dedication to his friends became one of the hallmarks of his young life.

As the years went by, Carlo grew up like most children of his age. In the mid-1990s video console games as well as small handheld devices became increasingly popular. Carlo played on these miniature screens, Pokémon being one of his favourites. At the age of eight he was given a video game console. Carlo soon realised that such games can become addictive and so he decided to limit himself to an hour a week. He was taken aback when some friends came to his home one afternoon and played with the video games. A row broke out and ended in a violent disagreement. He decided to avoid such occasions in the future and preferred to meet his friends for sporting activities and hikes.

Carlo enjoyed the cinema and television programmes. When the Catholic television station SAT2000 launched in 1998, he became an enthusiastic follower. The station broadcast Mass, religious ceremonies, documentaries and discussion programmes which fascinated him. In particular, he followed a broadcast on Saturday evening which prepared people for Sunday with a commentary on the readings to be read the next day at Mass. Yet that did not prevent him from watching cartoons, especially *Spider-Man*, which he particularly enjoyed, or programmes about wildlife and animals.

Carlo was particularly inspired by the documentaries on the lives of saints. As most young children like tales of heroes and heroines, Carlo saw the saints as spiritual heroes and observed that every Christian is "a saint in the making." During the year-long Jubilee to celebrate two millennia of Christianity in 2000, Carlo watched many ceremonies which were broadcast live from Rome. The station also broadcast the visits which Pope John Paul II made throughout his 26-year pontificate, 146 within Italy and 104 abroad. Covering over a million kilometres, these journeys were more than the visits made by all his 264 predecessors over two thousand years. Carlo had great respect for the elderly pope, debilitated by Parkinson's disease, who continued to inspire vast numbers of young people in their Catholic faith.

All the time, Carlo's character was maturing. He read daily from the Bible, in particular from the New Testament. He set himself the task of reading the entire Bible, a daunting undertaking even for a Scripture scholar, let alone a schoolboy. Yet he became extraordinarily familiar with the sacred Scriptures, and his notebooks contain lengthy meditations on various elements of biblical teaching. Many of these were developed from the pre-Confirmation classes which he attended at the ages of eleven and twelve. While most of the classmates who were preparing to receive the sacrament of Confirmation simply attended the classes held in the parish centre, Carlo embraced the opportunity of deepening his knowledge of the Bible and of his Catholic faith. Since receiving his first Communion at the age of seven, Carlo availed of the sacrament of Penance and Reconciliation every week.

On 24 May 2003, in the parish church of Santa Maria Segreta, Carlo, along with several school companions, received the sacrament of Confirmation from Monsignor Luigi Testa, former private secretary of Cardinal Carlo Martini. As a means of showing gratitude for the sacrament which he had received, Carlo volunteered to help as an assistant catechist to prepare younger children for the sacrament of Holy Communion in his local parish of Santa Maria Segreta. This required assisting at a weekly preparation class in the parish which young children attended for a year or two before they received Holy Communion for the first time. The notes that he had taken from his own preparation were to come in useful as he prepared to teach others. At one of his first classes teaching younger children, he discovered that few of them possessed a Bible. He visited a number of neighbouring churches before he found one which had a number of disused Bibles. The sacristan gladly parted with the Bibles, happy to see them once again in use.

3.

The young teen took his duties as a junior catechist seriously and tried to live simply. Although his family were wealthy, Carlo grew increasingly impatient with their constant gifts. Christmas and birthdays were accompanied by presents but he firmly rejected gifts of things which he did not need. Each year in May, to celebrate Carlo's birthday, the family went to Gardaland Resort near Milan. Carlo always insisted on bringing friends to share the outing.

Antonia was a self-confessed shopaholic and enjoyed buying items for the family, but in particular for her only child. When she bought him a pair of sports shoes, she tried to buy two, in different colours. Her son became irritated and insisted on just buying one pair. One day he accompanied his mother to a shoe shop to buy a pair of sneakers. His mother asked the shopkeeper for two pairs, but Carlo objected immediately, asking his mother instead to donate the money to a poor person. "I don't need two pairs of shoes," he protested. "I only have two feet!" Reluctantly his mother gave in, hoping that another occasion would arise to visit the shop. But she also knew that Carlo could be extremely stubborn.

Although he generally favoured a simple way of life, in reality, he appeared to be fortunate in coming from a wealthy family. He certainly lacked nothing. Nor was he indifferent to some of the luxuries around him. Since he was a very young boy, he collected small model cars and in his early teens he took an increasing interest in cars. But he was always on his guard against excess.

Antonia noted her son's purity, his desire to please God. "I want to be for God, not for myself," he noted in his diary. The Italian phrase 'non io ma Dio' – not me but God – occurs regularly in his writings and became his favourite motto. The television was often on at home, especially before the evening meal when many Italians watched the news bulletins. Occasionally, as he passed in front of the television he noted something which he found embarrassing or recognised as unsuitable for a child his age. Italian television often broadcast images of scantily clad women to advertise products. Carlo found these images disrespectful to women. His embarrassment grew deeper as, like other children his age, he emerged awkwardly into his teens.

While it might be easy to form the impression that Carlo was almost too good to be true, there are plenty who remember his mischievous and giddy side. From his earliest years, when he got a video camera, he recorded plays with his four dogs and two cats as protagonists. With his vivid imagination, he wrote out short plays in which he invited his friends to take part, and in which he also acted. At parties, he recorded the festivities with his friends so as to preserve memories of the day. He participated in school plays and other events happily, singing, dancing and fitting in with the roles assigned by the teachers.

The teachers in the various schools that Carlo attended recall him as a cheerful young man whose main defect was that he continuously talked in class. Reprimands to be quiet failed, but he also took part in serious debates. During a religion class, the classmates discussed abortion with the teacher. Carlo affirmed the Catholic position that procured abortion is not permitted and is almost invariably against the moral law.

There were two groups to which Carlo formed a particular attachment. As a young boy, Carlo attended the Church of the Sacred Heart close to the central train station, administered by the Capuchin friars. These religious brothers and priests follow the Rule of St Francis of Assisi and part of their charism is their care for the poor. To this end, in 1958, they founded the Work of St Francis, a hostel which provides food and the personal needs of the district's poor. Carlo asked one of the friars if he could become a volunteer to help the people who attended the centre each day. Because of his youth, the friars refused him permission, telling him that when he was older he could come and help. The friar did not believe that the young boy could cope with the harsh reality of life on the streets of the city which many people endured. Despite this, Carlo continued to visit the friars, asking if there was some way in which he could be useful, and finally he was allowed to help in the preparation of food and sorting out clothing for people in need. One of the elderly friars, Giulio Savoldi (1928–2010), recalled his visits:

"He was a serene young boy, with a bright face, open to everything that is good and beautiful, certainly fortified by the Spirit of the Lord. He was very sensitive to the poverty and suffering of others, and, as best he could, he wanted to contribute to soothing the pain of those who were less fortunate than him. One day, I recall, he brought me his little saving box and gave me the contents to help the most needy children."

There was better luck awaiting with the Missionary Sisters of Charity, which had been founded by the well-known Albanian nun St Theresa of Calcutta. Four nuns of the congregation had arrived in Milan in 1983 and begun to provide food and clothes for the poor of the central district of Milan. Each day the sisters brought food to people near the central train station. Soon a food kitchen provided meals for 150 people, while a refuge was set up for 50 women and children. This help was offered by the sisters to people of all races and religions. Their secret was to inspire helpers to join their tiny number and so provide an efficient service to a large number of people. The meals were prepared in a small kitchen and provided every evening. Secondhand clothes donated to them were sorted according to sizes so that a clothes bank was available to everybody in need. Carlo was just one of the large number of helpers who donated a few hours every week to lend a helping hand. He was remembered for his boundless energy at arranging the clothes in the depository and his cheerfulness. He was also one of the youngest volunteers and the other helpers were impressed by his energy and enthusiasm.

Carlo had a particular empathy for older people. During his vacations he enjoyed speaking with his relatives and, when at home, he regularly volunteered to run errands for some of the elderly neighbours who lived in his apartment complex.

In 1993, the internet, which had been invented ten years earlier, was made available to the public. The world wide web became enormously popular, and fuelled a phenomenal production of personal computers. The Acutis family was one of the first to purchase a computer for domestic purposes and also a subscription to the internet. The computer had a screen and separate keyboard while the motherboard and internal drive was housed in a separate casing. An external modem linked the computer with the web. Connections via telephone cable were slow, expensive and unreliable. Carlo immediately became fascinated by the new technology and quickly learned to type. He purchased CD-Roms, discs which allowed access to various graphic design programs and a new world of communications.

In late August 2002, Carlo travelled to the seaside town of Rimini on Italy's eastern coast, where he participated in a gathering of young Catholics organised by a Milanese priest, Don Luigi Giussani. Since the first international *Meeting for Friendship Among Peoples* in 1980, the international gathering known as the Rimini Meeting has attracted tens of thousands of people from across Italy and abroad to attend seminars, workshops and exhibitions on Catholic themes. As he wandered through the marquees and makeshift buildings, Carlo had the idea of organising an exhibition on the Eucharist – in particular, Eucharistic miracles which had been recognised by the Catholic Church. The exhibition would take two forms, one digital and available online, while the second would consist of printed panels which could form a travelling exhibition. Carlo thought that such a project might persuade people who did not appreciate the Eucharist and help their faith. He returned home to progress the project, which would take up much of his free time over the next two-and-a-half years. Enthused by the project, Carlo convinced his parents to take short vacations to some places connected with alleged Eucharistic miracles so that he might take photographs. He found information on the Eucharistic miracles on the internet and, with the help of his mother, summarised these into short accounts of each sanctuary or shrine associated with the Eucharist.

As he researched the miraculous accounts, Carlo became increasingly fascinated by what he read. In particular, he was particularly interested in an account of the alleged 'miracle of Lanciano'.

According to a late sixteenth-century tradition, a Basilian monk had doubts about the presence of Jesus while celebrating Mass in the Italian city of Lanciano sometime in the eighth century. The tale recounted how the host turned to flesh and the wine in the chalice coagulated like blood. The monks at the sanctuary of Lanciano in eastern Italy claimed that the relics from this miracle had been in their care for centuries, although no historical documentation supported the claim prior to 1574. It was strange that no cult would have arisen, or documentation found to exist over the intervening 900 years. Tests carried out in 1970 confirmed that the membrane was cardiac and the blood was human. But there is no dating of the tissue and there is nothing attaching the human remains to a Eucharistic miracle. It seems more likely that the 'relics' and the story were created, possibly with the macabre use of human cardiac membrane, to stoke belief in the Eucharistic presence of Jesus among a largely illiterate populace.

Reading this and accounts of other Eucharist phenomena, Carlo made a list of alleged miracles connected with the celebration of Mass in an effort to verify those which he believed had scientific evidence and those which were clearly fraudulent. He had worked on several school projects on a variety of subjects, so he approached this challenge in the way he addressed every project. He searched the internet to find accounts of alleged miracles connected with the Eucharistic bread. For centuries Christians has sought relics of Jesus, from the wood of the manger to the wood of the cross on which He died, leading to a brisk trade in forgeries to obtain the money or trust of an unsophisticated populace. The sixteenth-century Reformation exposed the wholesale exploitation by unscrupulous members of the Church, invariably with a lucrative goal. Lacking any relic of Jesus, many made claims that a consecrated host had turned to the flesh of Jesus and the wine had turned to blood.

While the Holy See often carried out investigations on such popular phenomenon, these were rarely accompanied by rigorous scientific testing. In recent years the Holy See has been slow to investigate miraculous claims but in 2024 Pope Francis issued a decree acknowledging "manipulation, damage to the unity of the

Church, undue financial gain, and serious doctrinal errors that could cause scandals and undermine the credibility of the Church." This was an understatement, and failed to acknowledge that in the past Church authorities were complicit in fraud. The document, approved by the pope, notes that some apparently miraculous events "at times appear connected to confused human experiences, theologically inaccurate expressions, or interests that are not entirely legitimate."

The collation of material gathered by Carlo offered an uncritical view of these Eucharistic miracles. The internet was still in its infancy when he began this work. Much of the information was gathered from inaccurate websites and inserted onto his website with photographs and brief descriptions. Carlo constantly updated his website, adding new material as he became aware of more mysterious, if not contro-versial, events. The Vatican document issued by Pope Francis was prepared in part to tackle the plethora of pseudo-supernatural claims which continuously spread across social media. Given the Catholic Church's long and controversial history of super-natural events, it is ironic that the Holy See is now obliged to intervene and tighten claims and assertions which were long left to the local bishop or religious authorities.

Had he lived, Carlo would have most likely updated and corrected the historical inaccuracies of the claims made by custodians of some shrines. Today his original panels, despite their clear limitations, are a remarkable testimony of his dedication to the Eucharist.

* * *

In the first months of 2005, the Catholic world followed the health trials of the 84-year-old Pope John Paul II. For more than a decade he had battled Parkinson's disease, while trying to guide the universal Church.

The pope had gained a particular place in the hearts of numerous young Catholics. He proposed a strict morality and challenged contemporary youth to remain faithful while exploring new ways of expressing their Christian beliefs. Every two or three years, Pope John Paul II met with young people for a few days in different parts of the world. These World Youth Days were attended by millions of young people, who spent several days together, attending seminars and gathering for social spectacles. For a man who had lived through the atrocities of the Second World War, these events brought enormous pleasure to the pope as he saw young people learn from each other and forge strong bonds of friendship.

The pope's days were clearly numbered. He was hospitalised several times with complications of his illness. Having survived the assassination attempt in St Peter's Square on 13 May 1981, the pope had continued his ministry with energy and enthusiasm until his late 70s. But age and illness were now taking their toll, and his physical clock was slowly winding down.

People from all over the world watched the pope's travails. Italian television, in particular, broadcast regular updates. The 14-year-old Carlo followed the pope's decline each evening on television and read the updates in his parents' daily newspapers.

The suffering came to an end in the late evening of 2 April 2005, when Pope John Paul II died. Archbishop Leonardo Sandri announced to the thousands gathered in St Peter's Square that the pope had "returned to the house of the Father."

The Acutis family followed the broadcast live and the subsequent preparations for the funeral, which was held the following week. Up to four million people paid their respects as the pope lay in state in St Peter's Basilica As the obsequies took place during school term, the family remained in Milan and watched the ceremony on television.

Two weeks later, the cardinals gathered in the Sistine Chapel in the Vatican where, on 19 April, underneath Michelangelo's great fresco of the Last Judgment, they elected Cardinal Joseph Ratzinger as Pope Benedict XVI.

In June of the previous year, Pope John Paul II had convoked a special year of prayer and study to the Holy Eucharist. Among the events was a Eucharistic photographic exhibition to be held in Rome in the spring of 2005. Carlo's Eucharistic project had been selected to form part of the exhibition and, in early May, the family travelled to Rome. When they visited the Vatican, the family joined the long queue to visit the tomb of Pope John Paul II in the lower crypt of St Peter's Basilica. Such was the enormous line of visitors and pilgrims that people were not allowed spend more than a brief moment in prayer before being bustled along by the custodians. Nonetheless, the brief visit made a significant impression on the young boy.

The photographic exhibition, on which Carlo had worked for over two years, was inaugurated on 5 May 2005 at the Athenaeum Regina Apostolorum house of studies. The invitation to participate and see his own work on display gave Carlo a sense of pride and satisfaction. He could hardly believe his luck to have had his work selected, having submitted the project in a competition organised by the Congregation for the Doctrine of the Faith to mark the October synod of bishops on the Eucharist. On the day of the inauguration, he met several cardinals. Among the officials working in the Congregation was Monsignor Domenico Sorrentino. The two shook hands and the cleric complimented Carlo when he discovered that he was the author of the Eucharistic panels. Just a year later, he was appointed by the pope as the new bishop of Assisi. How could he have had guessed that fifteen years later he would witness Carlo's beatification and that his diocese would host tens of thousands of pilgrims who would come to pray at the tomb of the boy who then stood before him, smiling broadly.

Websites were a passion for the young Acutis. Had he grown into an adult, he might well have followed his mother's profession in publishing, specialising in websites. As he finished the Eucharistic miracles exhibition, he immediately began a similar website dedicated to the Virgin Mary. At the start of the school year in 2006, the idea came to him of a website on the lives of the saints. There seemed to be no end to his energy and enthusiasm. But indeed, the end was already looming into sight.

4.

In September 2005, Carlo began his secondary education at the prestigious Leone XIII Institute, a school administered in Milan by the Society of Jesus, a fraternity known as the Jesuits. The Society of Jesus is particularly dedicated to the eduction of young people. Today there are over 3,450 Jesuit schools and 226 Jesuit universities and institutes of higher education across the globe.

The Jesuit order was established by St Ignatius Loyola, a Spanish nobleman and soldier who decided to become a priest and dedicated himself to the reform of the Catholic Church in the mid-sixteenth century. With a small band of like-minded priests, Ignatius and his first companions dedicated themselves to the education of the young. In 1517, an Augustinian friar and university lecturer, Martin Luther, had challenged authorities in the German town of Wittenberg to discuss the present state of the Catholic Church. In a series of 95 thesis, Luther had exposed the corruption of the papacy and papal court, as well as the superstitions fostered by unscrupulous churchmen who took advantage of people's unsophisticated faith. Much of this exploitation was aimed at obtaining money from people.

The pope of the period, Leo X, grandson of Lorenzo the Magnificent of the wealthy Florentine banking family the de' Medici, was little interested in the objections raised by the German friar. But Luther soon gathered political support, leading to civil unrest and violent clashes throughout the country. Twenty-seven years were to pass before the bishops of the Church assembled in the town of Trent, at the foot of the Alps, to address Luther's doctrinal and ecclesiastical challenges. By then, Europe was entering a period of wars caused by the religious divison between Catholics and Protestants.

It was during this period that Ignatius offered his service and that of his companions to the pope in the hopes of combatting the challenges through education. The early Jesuits set up colleges for training priests and missionaries not only in Europe but also in Japan, China and India.

In 1564, the archbishop of Milan, Carlo Borromeo, invited the Jesuits to set up a school in Milan for the education of the youth. Twelve years later the school established at Brera offered classes in Latin, Greek, Hebrew, Italian, mathematics, physics and the sciences. The school closed with the temporary suppression of the Jesuit Order in 1773, and it was not until 1893 that a new school was opened and named in honour of the then reigning pope, Leo XIII.

The original school was an imposing brick building, but it was partially rebuilt and expanded in 1950 and now provides classes for children from the ages of 4 to 18. The school continues to be one of the most sought-after educational establishments in the city of Milan, continuously improving the education and sporting faculties offered to the students.

The school, based in central Milan, has more than 1,400 students and 140 teachers. Many alumni of the fee-paying establishment go on to play important roles in Milanese and national society.

Carlo was naturally excited to join such a prestigious school and, although he would miss his friends at his former school, he looked forward to making new acquaintances. With his genial disposition, he made friends easily and rarely gave or took offence from his contemporaries. Although he was particularly good at science and mathematics, he enrolled in the classical lyceum, which emphasises the humanities and languages. His knowledge of English, learned in particular from his father, was a significant help. He continued to develop his interest in computers and taught himself complex coding. When he was nine years old, Carlo's mother had bought him coding textbooks used at university, which he quickly mastered.

Within a few weeks the students had come to know each other and settled into their first-year routine. Carlo's facility and expertise with computer technology was noted, and soon classmates turned to him for help in preparing eighth grade final presentations. Several years later, many students recalled how he quietly befriended his peers, who found settling into a new school difficult, and encouraged them to persevere with the new subjects and other challenges. The Jesuit chaplain, Fr Roberto Gazzaniga, observed Carlo during break times:

"He happily walked around the hallways throughout the two floors of the school during the mid-morning break, looking to connect with both students and faculty. He was often joined by classmates who, had he not stepped in, would have spent the break at their desks or nearby, waiting for the bell alone."

This did not always win Carlo friends. There were petty jealousies, and he became, from time to time, mired in disputes. However, he had no patience with his fellow students who excluded others from their circle. His challenge was to find a way which would engage them and encourage them to welcome others. "I never saw him get angry even when provoked," recalled a classmate some years later. Another remarked, "if you were in a bad mood, and spent time with him, it would fade away." Another observed, "his kindness and his welcoming attitude, including when it came to inviting friends and schoolmates to his own home, gave you the feeling that he was never just listening to listen, but rather was really interested in people."

The Jesuits encouraged the students to engage in volunteer work in their neighbourhood or in the city itself. There was a small committee made up of parents, adults and students. Carlo joined the committee and, with his knowledge of computers, was able to devise strategies to streamline the work. Over his first summer, he used a professional software, called Dreamweaver, to develop a website on which he presented various opportunities for volunteering to fellow students. Participation in this group gave him confidence and slowly he developed his skills both as an innovator and leader.

In addition to the academic activities, Carlo joined in the various sporting activities organised by the school, and, in his spare time, he taught himself the saxophone.

To his special satisfaction, Carlo's mother began to study theology and the two thus developed another bond which united them.

Each year, during a school break in February, the Acutis family made a short trip abroad. In 2002 the family visited Portugal, and the following year travelled to France. On the last foreign trip in February 2005, this time made by car, Carlo's grandmother Luana joined the vacation, along with the latest puppy, Briciola. The visit to the Marian shrine of Lourdes, in the French Pyrenees, was suggested by Carlo as he had been fascinated by the story of the apparition there since his earliest childhood.

On 11 February 1858, 14-year-old Bernadette Soubirous and her sister and a friend were collecting wood for a fire near Lourdes when they claimed to have seen a mysterious woman in a grotto close by the river Gave. The children were mesmerised by the strange woman, who simply looked at them in silence. When they told their parents, the children were forbidden to go back to the area. Bernadette continued to visit the grotto on eighteen occasions until 16 July of that year. The local parish priest was skeptical of the young girl's claims but when the figure identified herself under the religious title of "the Immaculate Conception" or the one immaculately conceived, he came to believe her. Pope Pius IX had proclaimed the dogma of Mary's conception without original sin just four years previously.

People were divided over Bernadette's claims, some accusing her of being a liar while others believed that the Virgin Mary had appeared to her. A church investigation decided in 1862 that the apparitions were worthy of belief and soon a church was built on the site. Four years later, Bernadette joined the Sisters of Charity, a religious order in the French town of Nevers. She remained in the community of sisters until her death in 1879 at the age of 35. In 1933, Bernadette was canonised by Pope Pius XI.

During the two days which the family spent at Lourdes, they visited the grotto where the Virgin was said to have appeared to the children, and on both evenings, they took part in the candlelight procession and recitation of the rosary. The short vacation concluded by visiting the Spanish cities of Burgos and Madrid.

On one occasion, Carlo's father suggested a visit to the Holy Land to see the place where Jesus was born, lived, died and rose from the dead. The trip seemed to be one that would appeal to his son in particular. But to his surprise, Carlo showed little interest. "Why go to the Holy Land when we can find Jesus in the nearest tabernacle?" Carlo asked. In his diary, he later wrote:

"We are much luckier than those who lived more than 2000 years ago with Jesus in Palestine. The apostles, the disciples, and the people of those times could meet Him, touch Him, talk to Him, but they were limited by time and space. Many

had to travel for miles on foot to meet Him … all we need to do is go the nearest church and we have 'Jerusalem' right outside our front door."

In the spring of 2005, the parish priest of Santa Maria Segreta asked Carlo and an engineering student to design and administer a new parish website. Within two weeks the internet domain was acquired and the site was ready.

One of the Jesuit priests teaching at the college asked Carlo if he could help with designing a website to encourage young people to volunteer for charity, especially those run by Jesuit schools and colleges. Together with a fellow student who shared his passion for computers, Carlo constructed a website designed to advertise the various opportunities available to young people who wished to help in the community. With his companions, he produced a short video, highlighting the role people with disabilities play in society. The video was submitted to an international competition and won first prize.

5.

During the summer of 2006, Carlo spent some weeks with his mother at his paternal grandfather's house in the luxurious seaside resort of Santa Margherita Ligure on Italy's west coast. As his grandfather had a boat, son and mother spent several afternoons exploring the beautiful bay around the Cinque Terre. One afternoon, his mother later recalled, while returning from Mass, Carlo asked what she thought about his becoming a priest. This was not the first time he had confided the idea in another, as he had already asked his grandmother. Aware that he was just fourteen, his mother simply said that, whatever profession Carlo chose in life, she wanted him to be happy.

The school year for teens in Italy starts in mid-September. The summer heat abates and families return from the mountains, hills and seaside. After the vacation at Santa Margherita Ligure, there was time for a brief sojourn at Assisi. Shortly before he left the town, Carlo called to visit the tomb of St Francis in the lower basilica, which stood on the slopes of the hill. He was disappointed that the church was closed for repairs and prayed briefly before the main door. He made a mental promise to return during the post-Christmas holidays. Returning to Milan, he spent a few days getting his books ready to begin his second year at the Institute Leone XIII. Although he had enjoyed his holidays, Carlo was looking forward to seeing his schoolmates.

Just a few days before the 2006 term commenced, Carlo complained of feeling tired. There was no particular reason to be concerned as children of that age often go through bouts of fatigue as the body grows and changes. During games he noticed that he bruised easily, but there seemed to be nothing to be unduly worried about.

Towards the end of September 2006, Carlo did not feel well but was reluctant to call attention to his discomfort so as not to worry his parents. On Saturday 30 September he returned from school at lunchtime complaining that he did not feel well and had a sore throat. Yet after lunch he and his mother brought the family dogs, Stellina, Briciola, Poldo and Chiara for a walk in the nearby park.

The next day, after Mass, the family went for Sunday lunch to a restaurant in the nearby town of Venegono. Having walked the dogs in the adjacent woods, they returned home. By evening he was running a temperature and he decided to go to bed early.

On Monday 2 October, he woke up, still with a temperature and aches throughout his body. His mother advised him to stay in bed for a day or two, believing that he may have caught the flu. As a precaution, she called the doctor who made a visit that afternoon and prescribed antibiotics.

Carlo continued to run a temperature and a headache, typical symptoms of the flu, which was in season. Several school companions had caught the flu. He kept himself occupied by working on the computer for a while. His mother tried to cook appetising and nourishing food, but he was unable to eat more than a few morsels. He had his dinner in bed. While his parents were in the room he suddenly said, "I offer my suffering for the pope and for the Church, so as not to go to Purgatory and go straight to Heaven." In the light of later events, the family interpreted this as a premonition of the change in his condition. A severe flu is not unusual, and, despite the unpleasant symptoms, his family were not unduly worried during these first days. They hoped that rest would see him over the worst while medications would control the temperature. Even his pets failed to cheer him up and he slept for long periods.

As the week progressed, Carlo's parents became increasingly concerned. On Wednesday 4 October, Carlo was due to present a website to the whole school, which the Jesuits had asked him to prepare on the charitable enterprises run by the order. There was an emphasis on the need to help people with disabilities. To his great disappointment, the presentation was made by some classmates instead. It was the feast of St Francis of Assisi, the national patron of Italy. Phone calls from his friends, telling him that the presentation had been successful, cheered him up considerably.

But the next day the doctor visited again, and said he suspected that Carlo had contracted mumps. A highly infectious virus, this explained the swollen neck glands and his general fatigue. Once more, there was little to do but allow time for him to heal.

Early on Saturday morning, the boy's condition worsened dramatically. When he awoke, he felt nauseous and weak, and unable even with his parents' help to go to the bathroom. Rajesh had taken the day off. With their son's rapid deterioration, Antonia and Andrea called his former doctor, who arranged for him to be admitted to the De Marchi Clinic, where he had previously worked. With great difficulty, Antonia and Andrea brought their son to the car and drove to the clinic. The doctor had phoned ahead and ordered blood tests.

On arrival at the hospital, his mother reassured him that he was in the best place and that the doctors and nurses would help him recover. He was placed in a wheel-chair and brought to the emergency room. Here all his vital signs were examined, and blood tests were ordered. His parents waited anxiously outside the emergency room, admitted only briefly to see their son.

In the later afternoon, one of the doctors met Antonia and Andrea in a side room. The results from the blood tests confirmed the worst possible news. Carlo was suffering from an acute form of leukaemia, cancer of the blood.

His stunned parents could hardly comprehend the doctor as he explained that the leukaemia caused tumours to grow rapidly throughout the body. The blood tests had confirmed that Carlo had a promyelocytic lukemia, commonly called

M3, which was regarded as almost one hundred percent fatal. The boy's parents refused to believe the diagnosis and wanted more tests done. The doctors added that the type of leukaemia from which Carlo was suffering had come silently. That explained how the symptoms had developed within a few weeks. The fear was that the loss of blood-clotting agents could lead to unstoppable internal bleeding. All the organs were at risk.

When Carlo was given the news shortly afterwords, he was shocked. However, anxious not to worry his parents, he tried to make light of the situation. "How can he tolerate this?" Antonia asked over and over as she watched the nurses try to alleviate her son's discomfort. She asked him how he bore the pain. "Mamma," he replied, "there are people whose sufferings are greater than mine."

Carlo needed to receive oxygen immediately and was brought to the intensive care unit. The procedure was unpleasant and caused him great discomfort. Antonia's mother had arrived in the early evening. Both women decided to stay in the hospital while Andrea went home to snatch some sleep.

Unable to rest or sleep, Antonia went at dawn to Mass in the Barnabite church across the road before returning to see her son. He had not slept either and was still in great discomfort.

The doctors made their medical rounds early in the morning and examined Carlo's vital statistics. The clinic was unequipped to provide him with the specialised care he needed so the doctors arranged to transfer him to the San Gerardo hospital on the following Monday. That hospital had a section which specialised in leukaemia in children.

An ambulance brought Carlo to the hospital at Monza while his parents travelled by car. His mother had arrived first and came to the door of the ambulance when it arrived. "Mamma," said Carlo, "I am not going to get out of here alive – be ready."

After registration, Carlo was admitted to a private room on the eleventh floor and further medical tests were carried out. Carlo asked if the chaplain to the hospital could visit to give him the sacrament of the Anointing of the Sick. The laying on of hands and anointing with blessed olive oil is an ancient tradition dating to the time of Jesus and the apostles. It is invoked on the sick to help them in their illness and to pray for healing. Father Sandro Villa, the hospital chaplain, came almost immediately and also brought Holy Communion so that the family could have the comfort and strength of Jesus in the Eucharist. Father Villa anointed Carlo on his forehead and hands with the holy oil.

Absorbing the shocking news was the greatest challenge Antonia and Andrea had ever faced. Word spread through family, relatives and friends. Carlo's phone lit up with messages of goodwill and wishes for a complete recovery. But being in the acute section of the hospital meant that Carlo was only allowed to see his immediate family members. The task of the hospital was to stabilise him in the hopes of bringing him to remission, if not a cure.

Carlo's parents were traumatised and the three prayed together. But he had little energy, and, despite his bravery, his condition continued to deteriorate. His legs and arms were alarmingly swollen, and he had severe pain in movement. Cryptically, Carlo whispered to his mother, "Don't worry – I will give you many signs." But Antonia could not understand what he meant.

 Suddenly the youth took his mother's arm and said he had a severe pain in his head. He closed his eyes and she told him to rest. But already he had lost consciousness and entered a coma from which he would not recover.

The family sat by his bedside, holding his hand and, despite the ventilator covering much of his face, stroking his cheeks and forehead. They were unable to comprehend all that had happened within the week. In the late afternoon, the nurses and medics were alerted to a change in his state as the machines controlling his breathing and oxygen saturations began to bleep. At 5.45 p.m on 11 October they turned to Carlo's parents and told them that their son had just died.

There was stunned silence, followed by uncontrolled weeping. After a while, the family left the room. They asked if they could donate Carlo's organs, but the leukaemia had made them unsuitable for recipients.

Even though there was no further brain activity, the respiration apparatus remained connected until Carlo's breathing finally stopped at 6.45 a.m. the next morning, 12 October. With little warning, Carlo's parents had to prepare for his funeral. An undertaker removed his body and arranged for his homecoming. Clothes, consisting of jeans, sneakers and a sports top, were provided.

That afternoon, Carlo was brought home and laid once more on his bed in his room. Word spread within hours and by evening the house was full with his family and friends. His classmates hung around the main door of the apartment block, unsure if they would be welcome to go up to where Carlo lay. The parish priest arrived to offer prayers of comfort with the family. Sobs and cries seemed to fill the whole apartment block before the area subsided into silence.

When the last sympathisers had left that evening, Carlo's parents tried unsuccessfully to sleep. The apartment was filled once more on Friday as people came to offer their condolences. Family members travelled from Turin and Rome. On the morning of Saturday 14 October 2006, Carlo's coffin was carried from his home and brought to the parish church of Santa Maria Segreta, where he had worshipped regularly.

The church was full of mourners. Neighbours, schoolmates, and friends filled the large building. The parish clergy and Jesuits from Carlo' school concelebrated the Mass, while his school companions provided some music. For the young people, the sudden loss of their companion was impossible to comprehend. The previous week he had been expected to inaugurate his website for people in need.

When the coffin was carried from the church, as a mark of appreciation the crowd outside broke into spontaneous applause, a common Italian tradition. The bells in the tower rang out the midday Angelus. Everyone embraced, family and strangers, as tears flowed.

Before his death, Carlo had said that he would like someday to be buried in the town of Assisi. There was no time to purchase a grave there, so the family had decided to place their son in a grave in the town cemetery of Ternengo near Biella, north of Milan. Carlo had visited the town often, as his father's grandparents had a house there. This would be his temporary resting place until a suitable grave could be purchased in Assisi.

The days following the funeral were a mixture of delayed shock, moments of comfort and disbelief. One morning his mother decided to put his room in order and, while tidying his desk, she switched on Carlo's computer. As she scanned the screen, she found home videos which he had uploaded. Watching some of them brought her both pain and relief. However, one video, recorded three months before his death, unnerved her. Looking into the camera, Carlo said, "When I reach 70 kilos, I shall die." Did the young boy have a premonition of his death? Did he suspect already that a serious disease was forming in his body? There is no way of knowing, but it seemed that Carlo was aware that something untoward was happening.

Carlo's wishes to be buried in Assisi were realised in the New Year. On 20 January 2007, his body was exhumed from the grave at Ternengo and brought by the undertakers to Assisi, where he was buried in the town cemetery. It was a quiet ceremony. For his parents, who continued to regularly visit their home in Assisi, there would be the bitter but comforting opportunity to spend time in prayer and meditation at the last resting place of their son. Little could they have imagined in those early days what was about to happen.

6.

In the weeks following their son's death, Andrea and Antonia Acutis received an enormous number of sympathy cards from family, friends and, surprisingly, from people whom they had never met. The cards reminded the childless couple of happy times, and evoked some merry memories. Emails also arrived, recounting events Carlo's parents had never known had taken place. The overwhelming message was of comfort but also a curious number of events which seemed almost supernatural. Many people related how they had prayed to Carlo, remembering his kindness and pleasant disposition. They felt that, if there was a heaven, Carlo might already be in that happy state and perhaps pray for them on earth. Some writers even told the parents that they had obtained favours which they regarded as supernatural.

For weeks following the death of her only child, Antonia spent hours each day in her son's room. While he was alive, she never interfered with his belongings. A tidy child, there was little to do to keep his room in order. But she found comfort in the silent apartment looking at his toys and his clothes, and reading the notebooks in which he had for several years jotted down his thoughts.

In the weeks and months following Carlo's death, the grieving parents received visits from family and friends who sought to comfort them at their sudden bereavement. But as time went on, the visits decreased and both Antonia and Andrea found themselves struggling in the lonely space of the loss of their beloved only child.

Although the visits to Carlo's parents and family decreased, his memory did not die. People remembered him and many prayed to him. Gradually a groundswell grew, and people recounted strange graces received through prayer to Carlos. When a memorial Mass was celebrated several weeks after his death, the local church was filled with young people. On 1 October 2007, less than a year after the death of Carlo Acutis, Nicola Gori, a journalist with the Holy See's newspaper, *L' Osservatore Romano*, published a brief biography with Paulist Press. He had heard about Carlo's short life from Antonia and had been impressed by the stories of his care for the poor and efforts to live a noble Christian life. In the press release, the publishers stated that they wanted to offer an uplifting account of:

"a teen of our times, like many others. He tried hard in school, with his friends, and he loved computers. At the same time, he was a great friend of Jesus Christ, he was a daily communicant, and he trusted in the Virgin Mary. Shortly before succumbing to leukaemia at the age of 15, he offered his life for Pope Benedict

XVI and for the Church. Those who have read about his life are moved to profound admiration. The book was born of a desire to tell everyone his simple and incredible human and profoundly Christian story."

The short book was an immediate success. Readers were impressed and inspired by the brief account. Many readers contacted the Archbishop of Milan, Cardinal Dionigi Tettamanzi. Some had stories of receiving a grace or help which they attributed to Carlo. Some were even calling Carlo Acutis a saint.

* * *

In the early years, Christians used the word saint loosely. According to St Paul, all followers of Jesus were to live saintly, or holy, lives. After death, many people were acclaimed as saints, even without formal recognition from Church authorities.

Over the centuries these procedures were modified and today's method of examining the lives of respected Christians follows clear guidelines. In the first phase, five years are required to pass before people can petition the bishop of a diocese to examine the life of a deceased Catholic. This prudent move allows either the memory of the person to settle, or devotion to grow. In the latter case, the bishop of the place where the person died appoints auditors who interview witnesses and other involved parties.

Once five years had passed since Carlo's death, Cardinal Dionigi Tettamanzi, Archbishop of Milan, was asked about the possibility of investigating the sanctity of the young boy who had died in 2006.

The cardinal was surprised to receive such a request and appointed a small group to carry out a preliminary investigation into Carlo's life. The investigation gathered some testimonies from teachers, family members and friends. It was an informal gathering of information, and the archbishop did not want to raise any false hopes.

The first formal step required the Archbishop of Milan to establish a diocesan committee to examine witnesses and documents. The next step required the bishop to speak with his colleagues in the Lombard region, who agreed to proceeding with a case.

Having read the dossier, Cardinal Tettamanzi gave permission to carry out a formal investigation into the life of Carlo Acutis. The young boy certainly appeared to have lived a virtuous life, in conformity with Christian teaching, in a remarkable manner. The only way to be sure that this was not the result of a small pressure group was to interview as many people as possible who knew Carlo well, and hear what they had to say. Only by gathering many testimonies, both negative and positive, could the authorities hope to form a rounded opinion. Thus, the negative and positive points of view had to be given equal weight.

On 12 October 2012, the sixth anniversary of his death, the Cause for the Beatification of Carlo was formally opened, according to tradition, in the diocese where he had died. Cardinal Tettamanzi presided over the ceremony, during which he commissioned delegates to gather information and testimonies from people who had known the boy. The authorities were aware of the rarity of investigating the life of a young person focused on personal sanctity. But this was an unusual case. Scores of people had already attested to the piety of Carlo Acutis; it was now time to investigate further and determine if what they had claimed was true and if it could be formally confirmed or exposed as a hoax.

The preliminary stages of the diocesan investigation gathered together the testimonies of many people who had been sincerely impressed by the sanctity of the young man. Each had been interviewed under oath and all had willingly attested to qualities unusual in a young person of his age.

Carlo's parents and family agreed to be interviewed by the diocesan theologians, as did many of his former classmates, friends and neighbours. What struck the theologians was that everybody had a positive view of the young boy and admired the way he helped people in need.

The investigative commission was headed by a Milanese priest, Monsignor Ennio Apeciti, an expert who had already overseen 33 causes for beatification. In early 2013, the results of the investigation were sent to the Congregation of the Causes of the Saints at the Vatican. On 13 May, the Holy See granted the Nihil Obstat, the required approval which stated that nothing prohibited the investigation from proceeding in Milan. Two days later, the first interviews took place.

Now the real work could begin. In addition to the small number of witnesses already interviewed, more had to be summoned. The interviewers were skilled in gathering information, but the reports had to be considered by psychologists. In addition, claims that people had benefited medically from Carlo's intercession had to be examined by a medical team. The medics were to examine the evidence dispassionately, and in particular to uncover if untrue claims were made.

All these interviews were carried out at the behest of Cardinal Angelo Scola, who had succeeded Cardinal Tettamanzi as Archbishop of Milan in June 2011.The diocesan investigation finally came to an end on 24 November 2016 when Cardinal Scola accepted the dossier, sealed it and sent it to the Vatican to be examined in further detail.

At the heart of the testimonies were a number of questions. Was Carlo sincere in his assistance of the poor and troubled, or was it simply to attract attention and admiration? Did he unite his family and friends, or did he cause division? Did he truly carry out his Christian duties or was this simply a façade? Did his life impact meaningfully on those who claimed to be impressed or affected by his sanctity?

The Vatican has a special office which looks after devotion to the saints. This office, known as the Dicastery for the Causes of the Saints, appoints nine theologians who read the interviews and, if they give a positive approval, the life of the deceased is examined in minute detail. As part of this process, the dicastery appoints a delegate whose task is to challenge any positive findings. For this reason, the delegate is often called 'the Devil's advocate' as he or she is charged with ensuring nothing dishonest happens. This period is referred to as the *cause*. The person is not expected to be without human fault: it is precisely because they tried to overcome failings that they are respected for living a good Christian life according to the Gospels and holy Scriptures.

If the theologians give their approval, a dossier is prepared for the pope. When the pope has read and prayed about the person, he meets with the cardinals to approve the next step, which is called beatification.

The entire process is akin to legal proceedings where both sides are subject to critical scrutiny. In particular, where miracles are alleged, medics offer dispassionate opinions. The medical experts are rarely Catholic; what matters is their competence in offering scientific evidence.

Pope Francis was informed about the cause for beatification of Carlo Acutis. The pope was impressed with the testimonies which were compiled and, on 5 July 2018, the pope accepted the judgement of the theologians and bestowed the title 'Venerable' on Carlo.

For beatification, a miracle is required, a token which proves that the person is capable of interceding with God. The miracle usually refers to the cure of a person suffering with physical or mental illness. The cure must be spontaneous and permanent. It must also be proved that the cure was obtained through the intercession of the person whose help was sought.

While miracles capture public attention, the centuries-old requirement for a supernatural event or healing seems out of step with the modern world. Many would prefer simply that the Holy See would examine the deceased person's life, to ensure that it was truly Christian. That would be sufficient to confirm exemplary sanctity. Many attest the occurrence of miracles, but the holiness of a prospective saint surely does not depend on inexplicable events.

Although there were many claims of miracles attributed to Carlo, one accepted by the Vatican authorities was the cure of a young boy from Campo Grande in southern Brazil, who was born in 2009. When Matheus Vianna was two years old, he was diagnosed with annular pancreas, a congenital condition which causes acute digestive problems. The medical team held out little hope that the boy would live long unless he underwent surgery to prevent constant vomiting and undernourishment.

When he was three, the doctors proposed the delicate surgery in the hopes that the boy, small for his age, would respond. Matheus' parents met with Fr Marcelo Tenorio, who suggested that they pray to God, invoking Carlo's help. On 10 October 2012, Matheus' grandfather brought the boy to a Mass at the church of Our Lady of Aparecida, during which he was blessed with a fragment of pyjama worn by Carlo. To the surprise of the family, the boy's involuntary vomiting stopped and gradually he resumed his normal life. The medical team examined him and discovered that his pancreas was functioning perfectly. An operation was no longer necessary.

Some years later the alleged miracle was reported to the Vatican authorities, who commissioned an examination of the medical records. On 14 November 2019, the Congregation of the Causes of the Saints gave its opinion of the apparent healing of the young Brazilian boy, which had seemed incurable and fatal. The alleged cure had been rapid and permanent. There was no medical explanation.

If, after the ceremony of beatification, the cult continues to grow, a further miracle is required before the final step. The end of the process is called canonisation, when the title 'saint' is officially conferred during a ceremony presided over by the pope. With this ceremony, the new saint may be venerated throughout the Catholic Church.

Cynics may have a jaundiced view of the way Blessed Carlo was proposed as a model for young people. Is this a way for the Catholic Church to attract young people? It is fair to say that it is, but, surprisingly, devotion to Blessed Carlo is not solely among the young. All generations appear to be attracted by this young boy who lived an ordinary life in an extraordinary way.

The same criteria required for canonisation applied for Carlo. While there was no shortage of reports of healing, not all could be followed. As in many trials, a sample case for a multitude was chosen.

After granting the title 'venerable', the practice of the Church requires that the body of the person to be beatified is examined and verified. Carlo's parents granted permission for the body of their son to be exhumed from the cemetery in Assisi and officially identified. This was done on a cold morning on 23 January 2019. Three months later, on 6 April, Carlo's body was brought to Assisi and placed in a specially designed tomb in the Church of St Mary, commonly called the Chapel of the Renunciation. A medieval tradition claimed that the church was built over the site where St Francis stripped off his clothes and handed them to his father. It was the decisive moment when he embraced poverty in a radical way, confiding himself to the providence of God.

On 2 April 2019, Pope Francis wrote a letter to the young people of the world, addressing their hopes and aspirations and acknowledging their daily challenges. The letter, *Christus Vivit*, takes its title from the opening words of the letter in Latin – Christ is alive. Having surveyed the world in which contemporary youth find themselves, Pope Francis recalled the life and example of Carlo Acutis, noting in particular his particular giftedness in the area of communications:

"Carlo was well aware that the whole apparatus of communications, advertising and social networking can be used to lull us, to make us addicted to consumerism and buying the latest thing on the market, obsessed with our free time, caught up in negativity. Yet he knew how to use the new communications technology to transmit the Gospel, to communicate values and beauty. Carlo didn't fall into the trap. He saw that many young people, wanting to be different, really end up being like everyone else, running after whatever the powerful set before them with the mechanisms of consumerism and distraction. In this way they do not bring forth the gifts the Lord has given them; they do not offer the world those unique personal talents that God has given to each of them. As a result, Carlo said, 'everyone is born as an original, but many people end up dying as photocopies.' Don't let that happen to you!"

The final step towards beatification came on 21 February 2020, when Pope Francis approved the miracle of Matheus Vianna and granted permission for the beatification to take place later that year in Assisi.

That very month marked the outbreak of the Covid-19 pandemic in northern Italy. Hundreds died in the first weeks and, as the virus spread across the globe, millions succumbed to illness. The world was caught in terror. There was no indication how long the virus would last. Scientists had little to offer apart from advising people to isolate and maintain hygienic practices. Within weeks, various pharmaceutical companies began to trial vaccines and within a year some were available.

Governments across the world restricted travel, even to the extent of advising people to remain within a short trajectory of their homes. When restrictions were relaxed in Italy, the Holy See gave permission for the beatification to take place in Assisi. The date was set for Saturday 10 October 2020, just two days before the anniversary of Carlo's death in 2006.

Although public gatherings were once more permitted, there were still restrictions on the numbers attending public events. There was still general fear about gathering in large numbers and only a crowd of three thousand attended the beatification Mass celebrated by Cardinal Agostino Vallini, the papal delegate.

As a precaution, everybody present wore face masks, to limit possible exposure to the virus. As space was limited within the Upper Basilica of St Francis, almost three thousand people filled the piazza outside the church, each prudently wearing a face mask.

At the beginning of the Mass, the papal approval was read out, and as the choir sang a hymn of thanksgiving, a white pleated satin curtain over the altar was lowered, revealing an oversized image taken from a photograph of Carlo.

In his homily, Cardinal Vallini recalled the reasons why Carlo could now be venerated locally:

"He was an average, simple, spontaneous, likable young man – suffice it to look at his photograph; he loved nature and animals, played soccer, had many friends his age; he was attracted to modern means of social communication, passionate about information technology and taught himself how to build programs to transmit the Gospel, to communicate values and beauty."

The cardinal admired Carlo's wish to attract as many people as possible to Jesus by proclaiming the Gospel first and foremost with the example of his life, for:

"it was precisely the witness of his faith that impelled him to successfully undertake the tireless work of evangelisation in the environments he frequented, touching the hearts of the people he met and fostering in them the desire to change their lives and draw near to God. And he did so spontaneously, by demonstrating the Lord's love and goodness with his manner of being and behaving."

Indeed, the cardinal continued, Carlo possessed:

"an extraordinary ability to witness to the values he believed in, even at the cost of facing misunderstandings, obstacles and at times even being derided. Carlo felt a powerful need to help people discover that God is near us and that it is beautiful to be with Him in order to enjoy his friendship and his grace."

Thus, he used "modern means of social communication, which he knew extremely well, particularly the internet, which he considered a gift from God and an important tool for meeting people and spreading Christian values." The internet was not "only a means of escape, but a space for dialogue, getting to know others, sharing, mutual respect, to be used responsibly, without becoming slaves, and by rejecting digital bullying; in the boundless virtual world we need to know how to distinguish good from bad." From this "positive perspective", the cardinal concluded:

"Carlo encouraged the use of mass media as a means of serving the Gospel, to reach the most people possible and to introduce them to the beauty of friendship with the Lord. For this purpose, he committed himself to organising an exhibition of the main Eucharistic miracles that have occurred in the world, which he also used when teaching catechism to children."

The rite of beatification solely permits local veneration. Only through canonisation may the cult be spread worldwide. For that to happen, a second miracle, following the beatification, must be examined and approved.

The public ceremony at Assisi introduced Catholics across the world to the life of Carlo Acutis, in particular the young generation at ease with social media. Within weeks, the story of the young boy had captured headlines not only within the Catholic community but also in the secular press.

7.

*E*arly on the morning of 22 May 2024, Pope Francis met with Cardinal Marcello Semeraro, Prefect of the Dicastery for the Causes of the Saints. During the audience, the cardinal gave the pope the results of investigations of some two dozen potential saints and martyrs. Among the list was the name of Carlo Acutis. The pope had already heard informally about the second miracle and told Cardinal Semeraro that he was particularly pleased that the Church would be able to canonise a young man, a contemporary of a new generation. The pope promised to convene a consistory of cardinals to make public his decision and to set a date for the canonisation. This is a formal step but by that evening, word had escaped. The bishop of Assisi, Monsignor Domenico Sorrentino, had already alerted Carlo's parents and although he was in Rome at a meeting of the Italian Episcopal Conference, he invited them to attend the midday Angelus prayer meeting in the Church of the Spoliation where their son was buried. The announcement would be formally made in Rome at the same time.

The news was largely kept confidential until the public announcement. Antonia and Andrea attended the brief midday prayer service before which was read the pope's decree by one of the Franciscan sisters. Afterwards, those present congratulated Carlo's parents while recognising the profound pain caused by the death of their son.

Antonia Salzano often recounted the reports of unusual healing or spiritual conversions that seemed to arrive by email almost on a daily basis. They came from all over the world. There were ever-increasing invitations to address groups, but also many emails, cards or letters came from people who, although they never had met her, felt they knew her through her dedicated service of keeping the memory of her son alive. The reports of unusual healings which she thought were worthy were periodically passed to the Dicastery for the Cause of Saints.

The second miracle which was accepted by the Vatican was the result of a spontaneous and permanent healing of a 21-year-old Costa Rican woman, Valeria Valverde, who suffered severe head injuries following a bicycle accident in Florence where she was studying at university. In the early hours of 2 July 2022, she was knocked down and was rushed to hospital to undergo an emergency craniotomy to reduce swelling caused by a brain haemorrhage. During surgery, part of the right occipital bone was removed to reduce swelling. The doctors held out little hope that the young woman would survive.

The medical team informed the family that the outlook was bleak as the surgeon was unable to prevent further bleeding. Valeria's mother, Liliana, was distraught. Her secretary spoke with her about the young Italian teen who had died suddenly in 2006 and both began to pray in desperation to Carlo. But nothing happened. The doctors continued to work to save the young woman. Word spread rapidly of the dramatic accident which threatened Valeria's life. Six days after the accident, on 8 July, Liliana travelled to Assisi, where she spent hours in prayer before the tomb of Blessed Carlo. Leaving a note close to the tomb, the mother begged for a miracle and made her way back to Florence to be with her daughter.

While her mother was in Assisi, Valeria began to breath unassisted and to recover. The hospital authorities phoned Liliana to give her the unexpected news while she was on her way back to Florence. The next day Valeria was able to move and began to speak. The medical team continued to monitor her progress and ten days later were able to allow her to leave the intensive care unit.

Diagnostic tests and a CAT scan on 18 July showed that the swelling had abruptly subsided, leaving little trace of the trauma. After three weeks of rehabilitation therapy, Valeria was discharged from hospital on 11 August. Her improvement was rapid and on 2 September mother and daughter visited the tomb of Blessed Carlo, convinced that his prayers had helped recovery and to offer thanks. As they spoke among their family and friends, the Franciscan friars asked if they could submit the apparently miraculous cure to the Holy See. The young woman readily agreed, little imagining that within two years her cure would be accepted as the required miracle for Carlo's canonisation.

On 1 July 2024, Pope Francis met with the cardinals to agree the date for the canonisation ceremonies of various people who were to be recognised as saints of the Catholic Church. He explained that he intended to hold the canonisation ceremony soon, but without setting a date. His intention was to celebrate the canonisation ceremony during the Jubilee Year of 2025, when over 30 million pilgrims were expected in Rome. The Jubilee tradition, which began in 1300, is celebrated every quarter century. The expection was that the canonisation would occur in the summer, when hundreds of thousands of young people gather for the World Day of Youth. For devotees of Blessed Carlo, the long wait to see their spiritual hero declared a saint seemed to be coming to an end.

8.

*P*eople often associate wisdom with age and life experience. This need not necessarily be so. Some people fail to learn and discern with the accumulation of the years, while others discover the meaning of complex mysteries at a relatively young age.

The observations and quotes attributed to Carlo come mainly from his mother, Antonia, who, in the years following her son's untimely death, has spread both his message and the richness of the Catholic faith across many countries. She has been both unselfish with her time and generous in sharing her personal memories of the son whom she loved and adored.

Antonia continues her role as mother even though her faith teaches that he may be venerated as a saint in heaven. For her, Carlo will always be her loving child. As devotion to Carlo and knowledge about him spread, Antonia was always liberal in her time, responding to letters, cards, emails and visits. She found it difficult to refuse invitations to speak at gatherings where an audience might listen to her. While those gathered may have hoped for a personal insight from the mother who bore the new saint or learned something interesting about his attitude to life, Antonia used memories of her son as a springboard to teach people about the beauty of the Catholic faith. Often, she began her address with a promise not to keep the audience too long, but, in full flight, she could match any prophet of the Old Testament. Her husband, on the other hand, has a very different character, being more reserved. Andrea is always at his wife's side, a quiet support as Antonia recalls moments shared with Carlo and sayings which remained in her memory.

Antonia jocosely remembers Carlo's insight and wisdom. Rather than her son, on occasion she felt that he was more like a father, imparting good counsel. He seemed to have the insight commonly attributed to the Buddha, Confucius or Socrates. Antonia often called him "my little Buddha, my saviour." His observations remained in his parents' memory, and both often reflected that it was Carlo who brought them to the Catholic faith, not the other way around.

As a young boy, family and friends often asked Carlo what he wanted to be when he grew up. It is a standard question which many people ask, searching for an insight into the mind of the young person. To this question Carlo gave an oblique answer. Rather than express what employment he intended to find, or studies he wished to pursue, he simply said, "to be close to Jesus, that is the plan of my life."

This disarming response may not have proved useful to the adults who asked the question, but it provided them with an insight about his priority in life. This was not simply a pious aspiration. From a very young age, perhaps as young as three or four, Jesus was clearly present to Carlo, God made visible in His humanity. The uncomplicated child's mind accepted easily the apparent contradiction of God who could be truly and fully human while retaining His divinity. The dichotomy has puzzled theologians since the time of Jesus and even the greatest minds have realised that they could only express an approximation of the truth of the mystery. The young boy was unable to cast his mind into the future. He lived within the limitations of his age, the natural reaction of any child when confronted about the future.

From the time when he could first speak and ask his mother for help, Carlo loved to visit the churches near his home in Milan. As Antonia brought her child in a buggy around the streets of the neighbourhood, Carlo insisted on entering the churches. As he grew older, he happily remained in silent prayer, absorbing the atmosphere of being in a house dedicated to God and sensing the omnipotence of God. The stories from the Bible which he asked to be read to him at bedtime painted in his mind the functioning of God's world and the place of humanity within God's creation. From this awareness flowed a sense of justice, that everyone deserves respect, and that people flourish when people live in peace with each other.

Carlo expressed this when he often repeated, "the only thing we have to ask God for in prayer is the desire to be holy." Holiness meant living a life of respect for God and for His creation. When there is imbalance or conflict, strife surely follows. Discord between humanity and God, or even between humans, clearly causes unhappiness. As Carlo grew older, he more often repeated this, especially when he taught younger children who were preparing to receive the sacraments of Penance and Reconciliation, and of the Eucharist. Holiness brought integrity and a sense of serenity, and these increasingly became visible hallmarks of his life.

This led the young Carlo to the Eucharist, which he regarded as the greatest treasure of the Church. Having received his first Communion at an uncommonly young age, Carlo fostered an ever-deepening understanding of the Eucharist, which he called his "roadway to heaven". When he began to study the history of the Eucharist in preparation for his internet project on the Eucharist, he read from an account by Justin the Martyr of the weekly Eucharist celebrated by Christians in the mid-second century. Justin describes the Sunday gathering of the community:

"On the day named after the sun, people who live in the cities and in the country gather for a celebration. Then the writings that the apostles have left or the writings of the prophets are read, as long as time allows. After the reader finishes his task, the presider gives an address in which he urgently admonishes the people to follow these excellent teachings in their lives. Then we all stand up

together and offer prayers. After the end of the prayers … bread, wine, and water are brought and the president offers up prayers and thanksgiving – as much as he is able. The people assent by saying 'Amen'. Then the things over which thanks have been said are distributed to all who are present, and the deacons take some to those who are absent. In addition, those who are well-to-do give whatever they wish. Whatever is collected is kept by the president, who uses it to help widows and orphans."[i]

It was this understanding that Jesus is present in His risen body which almost over-powered Carlo. "The Eucharist is the path to heaven," he was fond of saying, trying to convey the ineffable treasure which lies within our grasp. "The more often we receive the Eucharist," he observed, "the more we become like Jesus and thus come close to heaven." That Jesus appears "hidden in a piece of bread" was not only a link to the Jewish Passover but "is creative, something that only God could do."

Carlo derived both energy and peace from his time in prayer before or after Mass. He sat quietly, occasionally reading a few verses from the Bible. "People who lie in the sun get a tan," he noted. "People who face Jesus become more like him."

Some of his well-known sayings Carlo repeated often, and people who knew him became familiar with his thoughts. Other observations were written in squared notebooks so popular with young people, or kept on his computer. Some

---

[i]   Justin the Martyr, *First Apology*, 67.

were random jottings while others formed part of his notes for teaching catechism to young children in his local parish of Santa Maria Segreta. Fortunately, these sayings have been preserved by his parents who discovered them after his death and continue to derive comfort from their son's words.

Carlo came to understand the Mass not simply as an act of praise and thanks-giving to God but also as the reenactment of the sacrifice of Jesus on Calvary. Traditional Catholicism laid emphasis on the steadfastness of Jesus who chose death rather than renounce His teachings. Jesus always said that He had come from the Father and would return to the Father. That came about through His death. The Holy Spirit was then unleashed on the world as a creative and redeeming force which sustains the followers of Jesus.

The oldest church in the world is a house that was converted into a place for Christians to meet somewhere between 230 and 250 AD. American archaeologists discovered the ruins in the ancient Roman town of Dura-Europos in Syria. The town was deserted during a siege by Persia in 256, and in time the location was covered by sand. The ruins remained undisturbed until 1931, when they were uncovered during excavations of the area. The complex consists of a baptistery, a church for the Eucharist and a third room that may have been used for the instruc-tion of people who wanted to become Christian.

For the first three centuries, Christians were regularly subjected to imperial persecution within the Roman Empire. While many worshipped discretely, it was hazardous for Christians to gather and celebrate the Eucharist openly, and many were killed by the Roman authorities. The practice developed of allowing people to keep the consecrated bread in their homes. In the early fourth century, Emperor Constantine not only became a Christian but also permitted Christians to build churches for worship. Several were endowed with imperial funds.

It was from the mid-fourth century that the practice of reserving hosts consecrated at Mass began. This was originally so that people could receive the Eucharist when no priest was available to celebrate, and especially so that those near death could receive the Bread of Life. Gradually, devotion to Jesus present in the Eucharist bread developed and the host was treated with the same respect as if Jesus was physically present. For Christians, Jesus was present in the unleavened bread. "When we bathe, we become tanned. When we sit in front of the Blessed Sacrament, we become holy", Carlo often repeated.

Over the centuries, Christians became divided, and their system of beliefs diverged. In the sixteenth century, Protestant reformers protesting at the corruption which had permeated the Catholic Church challenged traditional teaching on the Eucharist. For some reformers, the bread was simply symbolic of Jesus' presence, while Catholic reformers firmly taught that the Eucharist was the true body and blood of Jesus.

Each day, before or after Mass, Carlo spent a short time in meditation before the tabernacle. "The more often we receive the Eucharist," he said, "the more we become like Jesus and have a foretaste of heaven." But the young man was also surprised that so many churches remained empty. "If there is a pop concert or a football match in the stadium then it is full and there are lines of people trying to get in. If people realised the miracle of Jesus' presence in the tabernacle, the churches would be full."

Shortly before he died, Carlo confided to his mother that he was pleased that, faced with a fatal illness, "I have not wasted one second that God gave me in doing things which would not please him." When his mother tried to comfort him, Carlo said, "If God is using me in some way to help people know how to live their lives, then I am content."

9.

Death always leaves a void. When Antonia and Andrea lost their son following such a rapid and sudden illness, they entered a long period of bereavement and disorientation. People did their best to comfort them, but the tiny trio was now reduced once more, as in the first days of marriage, to a lonely duo. Their memories of happier days sometimes provided comfort, while other days seemed to overwhelm them with bitter nostalgia and anger.

Comfort was not lacking and, as the weeks turned into months, the memories of Carlo, rather than fading, appeared to grow stronger. His mother, in particular, was prone to vivid dreams and sought solace in them. When the acute period of dolorous bereavement abated, Antonia and Andrea tried to have another child. Months passed to no avail. Antonia went for clinical tests to see if there was any impediment which could be removed, but there was nothing to prevent her having more children. Yet, nothing happened. One night Antonia dreamed that Carlo appeared and assured her that she would become pregnant and would have children. But almost four years were to pass before the dream became reality.

In early 2010 Antonia became pregnant and on 12 October, four years to the day of Carlo's death, she gave birth to twins, a boy and a girl. The parents named the girl Francesca, in honour of St Francis of Assisi, and the boy was called Michele, in honour of St Michael the Archangel, to whom their late brother had a great devotion.

Although now a mother once more, Antonia's memories of Carlo continued to shine. Indeed, she dedicated more time to the countless people who contacted her through various means who wanted to speak about her son. Perhaps the early years were a means of dealing with her unnatural loss. There were unending phone calls from ever-increasing distances. Emails arrived daily, along with cards and letters. These communications often carried invitations to speak to groups about her son. She had to decide would she refuse them all, or would she accept them and thus share the memories of her time with her son.

There was never any doubt what her choice would be. Antonia is a gregarious person and readily engages in conversation. In the years following the death of her son, Antonia travelled regularly to meet groups and encourage their faith by speaking of Carlo's faith. Antonia speaks French, English and Spanish in addition to Italian, a gift which allows her to communicate with relative ease.

By contrast, Carlo's father Andrea is a quiet person. Friends and family always noted how he listened to his wife as she spoke passionately about their son. While Antonia accepted the growing stream of invitations to speak, many of which required considerable travel, Andrea continued his professional work as head of the family company. But when his wife needed his presence and support, he was always present. However, by disposition he is reticent and reserved. During an interview in 2023, Andrea admitted that he regretted that he did not know his son as well as Carlo's mother. His work commitments were substantial and required much of his attention, and he was often obliged to travel. "But in the end, money and goods are not as important as love." In an interview given in June 2024 to the online newspaper *L'Identità*, Andrea recalled how his family were startled when Carlo broached the idea that he would like to be a priest when he grew up. Yet for Andrea, his son was admirable in the way in which he lived his life, helping his schoolmates and friends as well as offering practical help to people who were in physical or mental need.

As a result of the many meetings which Antonia addressed, she decided to write her own book on her son. She provided many intimate details of her son's life and points of view while also expanding her developing Christian faith and the parts of Catholicism which she found important and wanted to share with others. The book contained as much about the Catholic faith as the life and death of her son.

Carlo lived a short life. The years of infancy held less interest to the public than the later years as he entered his teens. His character was forming, as was his personality. One of the most revealing interviews with Antonia was that given to *La Stampa*, the Italian newspaper, which was published on 24 May 2024. The interviewer had not asked the usual questions that arose in groups, but probed her feelings in the face of bereavement and loss.

To these questions Antonia gave spontaneous and transparent responses, allowing the reader to see into her heart and glimpse how she has handled the greatest loss a mother could experience. With self-depreciation, which is common in the Italian sense of humour, Antonia observed, "He may be my son but sometimes I feel that I'm his secretary!" In a later interview given to the same newspaper on the day Pope Francis announced that Carlo would be declared a saint by the Church, she added, "He carries out his mission from Heaven, but I am his megaphone on earth!" As parents, Antonia and Andrea reflected on their unique role:

"We are extremely happy and not only for our own sake. We are happy for those who follow Carlo in their spiritual journey as well as in the key points of his life; his care for people near to him, whether they be poor, migrants, children suffering from bullying, the elderly or anyone in any kind of difficulty."

The question was asked how his 10-year-old brother and sister, Michele and Francesca, would react to the proclamation of their brother as a saint. "They understand that God is doing many things, but this does not take from their everyday life, which is the life that most of their age group have." They followed the example of the older brother, whom they never met, a unique sensation as they watched the progress of their sibling towards beatification and canonisation.

Devotion to Carlo has increased enormously since his beatification and the announcement of his canonisation. His family and friends continue to remember him with great affection while hundreds of thousands have learned about him through books and social media.

On the second anniversary of his beatification, the Carlo Acutis Soup Kitchen was inaugurated in Assisi in October 2022. This centre is run in conjunction with the Pope Francis Centre for the Poor attached to the Basilica of Santa Maria degli Angeli. A former convent beside the Holy Spirit School at Absecon in New Jersey, USA, dedicated to hosting young people who wish to spend time in prayer, was opened in October 2022 and named after Carlo Acutis. The first stained-glass window featuring a full-size portrait of Carlo, wearing a rucksack and carrying a mobile phone, was unveiled at the Church of St Adhelm at Malmsbury in England in 2022, just two years after his beatification. An article on the window, published in the influential newspaper the *Daily Telegraph*, brought the English boy to the attention of tens of thousands of British readers. The Blessed Carlo Acutis School in Cheshire in the United Kingdom was named in honour of the young English saint. In September 2023, a university residence dedicated to Carlo was opened in Stadera, in the heart of Milan, to serve 114 students from thirty nations, and permits those with limited opportunities to obtain third-level education. Carlo's family have sponsored many charitable acts to help people in need. Devotion to the young boy continues to grow in large part due to social media and the internet with which he was so familiar.

The exhibitions which Carlo designed have continued to fascinate people. While the websites are available online, thousands of parishes, schools, universities and prayer groups across the world have hosted the travelling exhibitions. The panels have been translated into several languages by volunteers and the panels have been shown on all five continents. Often saluted as a young computer genius, new websites dedicated to Carlo's story regularly appear.

10.

Many of the world's great religions encourage pilgrimages to holy shrines. The town of Veranasi, the City of Light in India, is on the banks of the Ganges river and sacred for Hindus. Muslims are expected to undertake the Hajj, a pilgrimage to the shrine of Mecca in Saudi Arabia, at least once in their lifetime. Christianity has a series of popular pilgrimage sites, including Jerusalem in Israel, Rome in Italy, Canterbury in England and Santiago di Compostela in Spain. The reasons for undertaking the journey in past centuries were varied. Some made the often-hazardous pilgrimage to fulfil a vow, others in expiation for a sin or crime, while for many it was simply an honourable means of leaving home and exploring the world.

Pilgrims identified themselves by amulets or tokens. Those on the way to Santiago wore a scallop shell to indicate they were en route and expected hospitality and protection as they travelled. Pilgrims to Rome and Canterbury wore miniature images of St Peter or St Thomas à Becket. Returning home, they often carried souvenirs of their pilgrimage to family and friends. Medals, pictures or other items allowed those who could not undertake the pilgrimage to at least share spiritually in the event.

In medieval times, churches and cathedrals displayed a collection of relics to pilgrims. The variety of relics was extraordinary, ranging from the bodies or bones of the saints to items which they touched. Often outrageous claims were made. The German reformer Luther stirred up greater ire, not from his challenge to translate the Bible from Latin into a language the people could understand, but from his ridicule and unveiling of the fraudulent claims of monks, friars and other ecclesiastics. In particular, he lambasted the claims of churchmen clearly intent on getting money from gullible and poorly educated people.

Luther mercilessly exposed the corruption of the Church. One church claimed to have a feather from the Archangel Gabriel, the Bishop of Mainz a flame from the Burning Bush of Mount Sinai, and Germany claimed the bodies of eighteen apostles when, observed Luther scathingly, Christ had only twelve.

While some clergy may have used relics and religious art to educate pilgrims, others took advantage of their superstitious nature. A robust industry in the selling of relics increased, in particular during the medieval crusades when knights returning to Europe from the Holy Land brought various items with them. It mattered little if they were genuine or fake.

The Reformation of the sixteenth century greatly reduced the fascination with relics, although many Christians still attach importance to the relics of holy people. The lives of the martyrs and saints continue to inspire new generations for their witness and efforts to live according to the message of Jesus, whom they acknowledge to be both fully human and fully divine.

There are three kinds of relics. The first is a part of the body of the blessed or saint, the second is an item, often a garment, which the venerated person wore or owned. The third class of relic is simply an item which has touched the body of a saint.

Such relics must be verified by the competent authority who can identify and confirm that the relic is genuine. Today unscrupulous people take advantage of the internet to sell fake relics to gullible people. Many are simply satisfied to have an image or a photograph of the saint which helps them focus their prayer and devotion. The saint may be an inspiration, but, above all, the saint is one who points towards Jesus who taught that He is "the Way, the Truth and the Life."[ii]

Assisi has been a pilgrimage centre since medieval times, when pilgrims began to visit the shrines of St Francis and St Clare, who are buried in the town. Since the beatification ceremony of Carlo in 2020, thousands visit the Church of the Renunciation where they pray before the tomb of Carlo Acutis. Assisi has a new saint.

When he died, Carlo's parents wished to donate his organs for patients in need, but his body was compromised. His heart is preserved in a reliquary in the Basilica

---

[ii]   The Gospel of John, 14.6.

of St Francis, while his body, largely incorrupt and dressed in navy jeans and a navy cotton jacket, is displayed in a glass-fronted stone monument. A silicone mask covers his face. For those unable to visit Assisi, a 24-hour webcam allows people from across the globe to see the chapel and tomb.

POSTSCRIPT

What would have happened if Carlo had remained in London, and grown up in the city? Would he have continued to live out his Catholic faith in such an active and generous way? Would he perhaps have become disillusioned by the scandals over clerical child abuse which destroyed the lives and shattered the faith of so many at the turn of the third millennium? Or would the malaise of atheistic secularism finally have eroded the religious sentiment of his soul? Or would his faith simply have diminished without reason? These are imponderable questions. The Christian faith in Europe and other parts of the globe has been gradually weakening for several decades, as people abandon their faith, or find it of little interest or assistance in their daily lives.

Many are critical of the manner in which the Church examined and then rapidly promoted the life of the young boy touted as "the first millennial saint." Yet in the face of increasing disaffection of young people and indifference to the faith, the enthusiasm and sincerity of Carlo Acutis seems to provide a beacon of hope for the future. If anything, the faith of this young man should be promoted and fostered to help his peers in their path towards maturity.

There is a further problem to consider. It is true that the young Carlo was unusual in that he prayed regularly, attended Mass almost daily and helped poor people. But he was not unique. There are other young people who successfully combine their school studies with their desire to help people in need and volunteer for charity. Perhaps not all of them are faced with sudden death, but not all are considered saints. Why choose this boy? Are these qualities really enough to be declared a saint? Carlo came from a wealthy family. He was indulged and appeared to have everything he could possibly want for in terms of emotional care and material goods. He literally never lacked anything and he never had to suffer deprivation, hunger or the suffering and affliction which scars the lives of billions of young people. Moreover, his life was sheltered, and he was never exposed to the hazardous world of illicit drugs, poverty, abuse or violence which damages so many young people. Can he really be considered a typical example of a young Christian who can speak to the people of this generation?

There are many uncomfortable questions surrounding not so much the life or even the death of the young London-born saint as the manner in which his cult grew and he was finally canonised. Social media was inundated with cynical responses and often vicious reactions to the news of the canonisation, dismissing the event as an attempt by Church authorities to use his life and death in a ghoulish manner. Cyber-bullying surged as devotees of Carlo were targeted by hate mail and posts. But the cult of Carlo grew up spontaneously, prompted by the recollections and memories of people, often those who lived difficult lives, who found comfort in the life of a boy cut down in his prime.

Young people who love their faith and derive spiritual benefit are often an underestimated number. Just as news broadly prospers on disasters, good news is under-reported. We more readily watch viral videos of people killed in an avalanche than children rescued from drowning. We already know the children are safe – what attracts our attention is how many were injured as tons of snow knock people from the ski slopes like matchsticks.

In Ireland, a young boy named Donal Walsh died in 2013 after four years of intense suffering with bone cancer. He was just sixteen. Donal was by no means unique. Too often young people are struck with serious and often fatal diseases. But before he died, Donal caught the attention of the nation by a short appearance on television.

Donal was born on 15 June 1996 in Blennerville in Tralee, Co. Kerry, on the southwest coast of Ireland. He was the only son of Elma and Fionnbar Walsh and had one sister, Jema.

Among his passions was sports, in particular football. He played Gaelic football with Kerins O'Rahillys club in Tralee and rugby with Tralee RFC. He was a normal child, bright, cheerful and polite. But his life journey was interrupted at the age of twelve when he was diagnosed with a cancerous tumour in his leg. Once he and the family had overcome the shock, they accepted that the only treatment available was chemotherapy and an operation to remove the tumour.

The surgeons were able to give Donal a prosthetic knee, after which followed nine months of chemotherapy. Although he was no longer able to play sport, he returned to the field nine months after his operation. Unable to play, he had trained as a rugby coach and was now able to help train teams.

The young players were in awe of the boy who had undergone such trauma at the beginning of his teens. Seeing him helping them with their physical training and exercises brought a sense of worth and satisfaction to their game and a respect for Donal.

But there was something else Donal wanted to do. During his rehabilitation at Crumlin Children's Hospital in Dublin, he had been a patient in St John's Ward. He became aware of the need to improve services at the hospital and for two-and-a-half years he campaigned to raise awareness of illness in young people and the need for better hospital conditions. The money he raised over thirty-two months went directly to improving St John's Ward, a charity which continues to help children and their families cope with traumatic illnesses.

Donal's fight with cancer was not over. During a routine check in February 2012, a tumour was detected on his lung. Surgery was required to remove both the tumour and a portion of the lung, and a further three months of chemotherapy was prescribed.

During this time, Donal had to remain isolated to avoid infection. One of his favourite things was to light a candle and pray. He loved to pray the rosary and the Divine Mercy devotion promulgated by the Polish nun St Faustina. These were fast and repetitive prayers; they took him to a place where he was always happy.

The following October, Donal received a virtual death sentence. His medical team met with him and explained that the cancer, despite all efforts to contain it, had spread throughout his body. There was no hope, short of a miracle.

Donal knew this and so he asked his mother for three things: to receive Holy Communion every morning, to die with a clean spirit and to get up from bed every day and go somewhere

Rather than withdraw into himself for the last remaining months of his life, Donal dedicated himself to the care of others, in particular, his peers. In April 2013, just weeks before his own demise, he appeared on a popular television show, *The Saturday Night Show*, broadcast on the state channel, RTE 1. In his introduction, the host, Brendan O' Connor, said "my first guest is 16 years old, and he doesn't expect to live much longer." He explained that Donal had been invited because he had written controversially about teen suicide in a recent edition of the *Sunday Independent* newspaper. In a brief article, he had expressed his anger at the choice some teens made to end their lives, a choice which had a devastating impact on their family and friends. Brendan quoted from the letter:

"I realised that I was fighting for my life for the third time in four years and this time I have no hope. Yet still I hear of young people committing suicide and I'm sorry, but it makes me feel nothing but anger.

I feel angry that these people choose to take their lives, to ruin their families and to leave behind a mess that no one can clean up.

Yet I am here with no choice, trying as best I can to prepare my family and friends for what's about to come and leave as little a mess as possible.

I know that most of these people could be going through financial despair and have other problems in life, but I am at the depths of despair and, believe me, there is a long way to go before you get to where I am.

For these people, no matter how bad life gets, there are no reasons bad enough to make them do this; if they slept on it or looked for help they could find a solution, and they need to think of the consequences of what they are about to do.

So please, as a 16-year-old who has no say in his death sentence, who has no choice in the pain he is about to cause and who would take any chance at even a few more months on this planet, appreciate what you have, know that there are always other options and help is always there."

Three teens had ended their own lives in his native County Kerry in recent months. He pointed out that he was fighting every day to live while they decided to take their lives. He did not want to judge them, but he believed suicide was not the solution to their problems. It was an impassioned argument, and while it could not do justice to the complexity of suicide, it allowed Donal to appeal to his own peers to pause and ask for help.

Donal died on 12 May 2013 and his funeral Mass was attended by over 10,000 people, including family, friends, sporting legends, politicians and school companions. During their bereavement, Elma and Fionnbar decided to set up a charity to continue his work. They visited schools in the area to encourage young people facing emotional or physical difficulties. For sick children, they fundraised to support a hospice for young people in Kerry. Their initial support raised over €500,000, but soon more volunteers began to fundraise to help young people with mental challenges and serious health issues.

Through Donal's short life and the generosity of his parents and sister, thousands have found a haven of hope and a place of respite. The calming comfort offered by Donal's message, #livelife, may not always bring enduring hope, but, over the years since his death, it has inspired countless people to channel their suffering and keep climbing a metaphorical mountain to find a better view and a place to rest.

The vast majority of young people pass through their teen years into early adulthood, slowly steadying themselves as they take their place in mature life. The early years can be turbulent and challenging to navigate. Yet the example of ordinary teens such as Carlo Acutis, Donal Walsh and the countless other role models whom they find in their circle of friends and acquaintances can help them explore their religious faith and draw strength to sustain them in the daily struggles and challenges which are part of life's journey. Often the true miracle is the way in which they confronted their death, and their memory, which inspires others.

This story began with two saints in London, one young and one old. St John Henry Newman lived a long life, dying at the age of 89. A prolific writer, he mused once that nobody had the same task in life:

"God has created me to do Him some definite service; He has committed some work to me which He has not committed to another. I have my mission – I never may know it in this life, but I shall be told it in the next."

Life is not measured in years alone, but in the simple achievements which bring fulfilment. Great or small, they belong to each human whom God has fashioned and nourished. Carlo, Donal and countless others found in their Christian faith seeds of hope and comfort. Their lives may not have been long, but their achievements have outlived them.

One of John Henry Newman's most popular prayers contemplates the end of life.

O Lord support us all the day long of this troublous life,
until the shadows lengthen,
and the evening comes,
and the busy world is hushed,
and the fever of life is over,
and our work is done.
Then, Lord, in thy mercy,
grant us a safe lodging,
a holy rest, and peace at the last,
through Christ Jesus, our Lord.
Amen.

PRAYER ASKING FOR THE INTERCESSION OF CARLO ACUTIS

O God, Our Father,
thank you for giving us Carlo,
a life example for the young
and a message of love for everyone.

You made him become enamoured with
Your Son Jesus, Making of the Eucharist
his 'Highway to Heaven'.
You gave him Mary, as a most loving Mother,
and, with the rosary, you made him

a poet of her tenderness. Receive his prayer for us.
Above all, gaze upon the poor,
whom he loved and helped.
Grant for me too, by his intercession,
the grace that I need …
And make our joy fulfilled,
placing Carlo among the Saints
of your Church, so that his smile
may shine again for us in the glory of your name.
Amen

(This prayer is followed by reciting the Our Father, Hail Mary and Glory Be to God).